D1442548

Flashes in the River

RUNNING THE RIVER

Flashes in the River

THE FLYFISHING IMAGES
OF ARTHUR SHILSTONE AND ED GRAY

Essays by Ed Gray
Watercolor paintings by Arthur Shilstone

WILLOW CREEK PRESS

Minocqua, Wisconsin

Portions of the text have appeared in Gray's Sporting Journal, Sports Afield, and The Dartmouth Alumni Magazine.

Published by WILLOW CREEK PRESS
         P.O. Box 147
         Minocqua, WI 54548

For information on other Willow Creek titles,
write or call 1-800-850-WILD

Library of Congress Cataloging-in-Publication Data

Gray, Ed
     Flashes in the river : the flyfishing images of Arthur Shilstone and Ed Gray / essays by Ed Gray : watercolor paintings by Arthur Shilstone.
         p.   cm.
     ISBN 1-57223-040-1 (hc : alk. paper)
     1. Fly fishing—United States—Anecdotes. 2. Gray, Ed. 1945- . I. Shilstone, Arthur.   II. Title.
     SH463.G68 1996
     799.1'2—dc20   96-6031
                                                     CIP

Printed in Hong Kong.

DEDICATIONS

For Mac Perkins, who opened the gate. And for Becky, who has made it a garden.

Thanks,
Ed

• • •

To my wife, Beatrice, whose valued suggestions help to make the nervous process of picture making a little easier.

With gratitude,
Arthur

CONTENTS

PREFACE 7
WINTER 15
    ALASKA 23
SPRING 45
SUMMER 65
    ATLANTIC SALMON 109
FALL 119

MOVING UPSTREAM

ACROSS THE RIVER, RISING

It was nothing
Next to what held us, what lay before us,
What couldn't be won or lost, but only spent ...
— *Denis Johnson*

"What do you think?" I asked Jeffrey. "Try to ease across, or floor it and blast right through?"

We were standing beside my parked car in the Dartmouth College land grant, deep in the woods of northern New Hampshire, on the wrong side of the Dead Diamond River two days after a sudden storm had lifted the river two feet, separating the car from the access road with a roiling surge of muddy, downhill water. Hour by hour in those two days we'd watched the river as it had inched fractionally back toward the graveled set of purling shallows it had been when we'd driven across it the day we'd arrived. Now it was time to go, and the current remained high, fast and strong.

Jeff Hills and I looked at each other, letting the situation work its way through. We were four days away from our third graduation together: high school, college, and now — almost — graduate school at Dartmouth. I'm pretty sure he laughed first, but it was close. "Yeah, right," he said. "I'll take pictures."

It was June 1971, and that was a much better answer than it seemed at the time.

We had come here, to the old North Camp at Hell Gate Falls, 13 miles back on a dirt road, with a week to kill between exams and graduation. We were 26 years old; behind each of us lay 19 years in scheduled schoolrooms and two years under written military orders, all of it focused toward obtaining a standard series of very specific certificates. We were about to be handed the last of them.

Assuming, of course, that we got back across the Dead Diamond River in time to get there.

The trip to the Grant had been god-mothered the previous winter by Jeff's wife, Marion, who had fallen hook, line and Mickey Finn for Professor Herb Hill's pokerfaced tales of unmolested northern wildlife that came nightly down to the river to drink and frolic among hungry trout in front of the rarely-occupied cabins of the North Camp. "The Hell Gate," he'd said, "is Paradise misnamed."

"We *have* to go there," said Marion. "It's got to be like the Garden of Eden." In the darkened sulks of New Hampshire's endless March, there was no coherent retort.

And so in June we went, the three of us taking the long drive north through an almost finished New England spring. With us in another car were classmates John Hemingway and Scott Philbrook, who brought along his girlfriend, a nurse. Marion was eight months pregnant.

Most Dartmouth students never see the 13,000 acres of the College Grant, never wade or fish in the two brook-trout streams that flow wild and unstocked through it, never wake to river fog and wood smoke in one of its hidden log cabins. The tract lies four hours north of campus, near the Canadian border and too far away to explore casually. It doesn't matter. Just by being there, the Grant adds dimension and promise to the unfinished lives of all Dartmouth's graduates, since the development of anyone's individuality is only as genuine as the number of selected paths is outnumbered by the ways not taken.

Not that Jeffrey and I had trod many of them, however. Our separate but comparable paths through both undergraduate and graduate school at

Dartmouth had been least-resistant all the way. His unscheduled two-year hiatus came after we were sophomores while mine waited until midway through grad school, when draft deferments were peremptorily erased by the peaking body counts in Vietnam. Jeffrey had, by then, finished his active tour in the Marine Corps and was back at Dartmouth, trailing me by the two years I was about to spend as a naval officer in Norfolk, Virginia. We caught back up with each other for that last year.

In our variegated wanderings during those eight years when one or both of us had been enrolled at Dartmouth, neither Jeffrey nor I had ever set foot in the College Grant. It had been there for us, of course, and we both had known it. Like certain corners deep in the library stacks, we just hadn't gone there yet. And like the books on those shelves, the revelations of the Dead Diamond River lay self-contained and waiting, indifferent to even the probability of our approach.

But approach we did, finally and as a sort of let's-try-it, we-don't-want-to-have-missed-something

reflex at what was certainly the end of our full-time association with Dartmouth. Through the gate camp entrance we drove, expecting nothing in particular and everything in general.

That's pretty much what we found.

Inside the Grant, the drive was a winding rough track through unbroken white pine, spruce, alder, hemlock and wild raspberries. Hushed as a church, it seemed to us; just the long, quiet sweep of the northern forest, the crunch of gravel under our tires and an occasional sparkling blue glimpse of the Dead Diamond River, flowing south.

The country there is by anyone's definition the big woods, especially so when you realize that when you are there you are already deeply into a nearly unbroken series of timbered parcels stretching from Vermont to New Brunswick. The College Grant has borders back in its hills but the trees don't know them, the wildlife doesn't honor them and you can't find them. Stay near the road, they had told us as we showed them our vehicle permits back at the gate camp.

Or near the river. It was June, the best month of the year for brook trout fishing. Jeffrey and I had brought our fly rods and waders. *In* the water was where we'd be, and all the way up the access road we marveled at the unbroken riffles and rocky pools of the Dead Diamond.

Today there are two newer log cabins at the Hell Gate, one on each side of the river, but when we drove up to the turnoff back then there were just the old green-painted frame shacks of the North Camp, and they were across the river from the road. A cable-hung, plank-slatted foot bridge swayed its catenary way over the sliding water below it while beyond, across a high-grass field, a winding muddy path angled uphill to the cabins themselves, 200 yards away. The six of us got out of the two cars and checked it out.

The bridge builders had wisely selected a narrow, high-banked section of the river over which to hang it, but the tradeoff was that long walk on the other side to get to the cabins. Ultralight packing hadn't been on our minds back in Hanover, as the multiple corrugated cartons of canned food and bottled beverages in the cars attested to. We stood there looking at the bridge, at the long awkward path on the other side, and then we looked at Marion.

"Hey," she said. "I can cross that."

We looked back at the bridge, and at the 10-foot drop below it. "Let's drive up a ways. See if there's another way," I said.

There was, a hundred yards up. A steep little turnoff from the road that slanted directly down and into the river, which was only 30 feet wide, gravel-bottomed and shallow. And on the other side, leading directly to the cabins was the unmistakable contour of a two-track road coming right out of the river across from where the little turnoff went in.

We didn't even hesitate. With Jeffrey and Marion inside, I drove the Chevy wagon across. The deepest part was only 18 inches, and the others followed in John's van.

With at least an hour's packing and hauling saved by the simple expediency of driving across the river, we were in high spirits as the last of the gear was stowed in the cabin. It was two o'clock on a windless, crystalline afternoon and Jeffrey and I decided it was time to find the trout.

"Move the cars back across?" asked John as we started to go.

"Nah," I said. "Just have to bring 'em back to pack up at the end, right?"

That not one of us, there at the fully-accelerated apogee of our academic learning curves, thought to raise the obvious objection to this plan seems only a little more silly to me now than it probably would have then, had it even occurred to me as Jeffrey and I went out with our fly rods in hand, moving upstream and heading in the warm, midafternoon sun toward the unseen storm to come.

Jeffrey and I were both new to fly fishing. We did know one basic concept, however: The trout are always facing upstream, watching ahead for whatever is coming while holding their own position in the current. That they can see you too, as you stand in the stream angling for them, seemed axiomatic to us.

The solution, therefore, was to stand behind them and cast upstream to where they lie. This, however, was a skill that we didn't own. Our alternative was to crouch upstream some distance from a likely location and swing a wet fly on a long line down and across the current near the unseen fish. Success that way, we'd already learned, is more a function of luck and quick reaction, requiring less talent but some concentration.

That's what I was doing, trying not to miss one of those bright little flashes in the river, a mile or so from the cabins and around a bend from Jeffrey, when the lightning struck.

What's the loudest noise you've ever heard?

No, this was worse. This was incomparable, in the way that a sudden, single, top-of-the-lungs scream in your darkened, quiet bedroom would jolt you heart-stopped awake more than 100,000 full-voiced football fans ever could.

The rain and wind hit a half-second behind the thunder-cannon, slamming me from behind and lifting instant showering wavelets up and off the stream around me just as surge after surge of hard, wind-driven pellets of rain slashed in sheets through the instant darkness. Lightning and thunder came strobe-lit and constant, inseparable, and in the woods on either side of the river trees began to fall, cracking and popping as the wind pushed them down faster than gravity could ever have alone.

In the middle of the roaring, hissing, pounding barrage, as bolts of lightning struck almost constantly in all quadrants, I was standing knee-deep in running water. But on both sides of the river trees were slamming down in darkness and at random, everywhere around me. Fear feeds on helplessness, and mine was intravenous, numbing. Complete.

And then it passed. Rumbling and bumping down the valley, leaving behind a darkened and dripping world of angular and broken spruces on either side of the river that still came past at the same height, but now flowing like flattened and dented pewter, surface gray as if its internal lights had been turned off.

With shivers that ran completely through me, I moved unsteadily downstream until I found Jeffrey, speechless, in the water and moving up to look for me. When the blast first hit, a huge spruce had gone down on the bank right beside him, lying there in the deluge still hinged with green wood to the stump where it snapped, and Jeffrey had climbed out of the river and gotten under the natural shield as other trees came down all around him. Together we headed back, walking on the road and stepping over and around the scores of trees that now lay across it.

The others had, of course, been inside the cabin, feet up around the woodstove, listening to the rain on the roof while the storm eased past. It had mellowed by the time it had got here, and no trees had gone down, as Jeffrey and I could see in the deepening evening gloom when we reached the Hell Gate. We came inside to the woodstove warmth and Coleman glow, and the story was in our eyes.

While we told it, outside in the darkness the river began to rise.

By morning, when we walked down to stare at it, our clever little fording place was now a doubled-in-width, sliding brown torrent of turbulent water that none of us dared walk part way into, let alone all the way across.

"Think it'll go down in time?" Scott asked.

"Going to find out," said John.

With no option, we waited, watching the river in the fine weather of the next two days and making little rock cairns on the bank to mark its receding progress. The day of departure came, and our now very careful monitoring of the water level told us that there was more water than when we first crossed, but we differed on exactly how much. We hadn't, after all, taken an initial measurement.

"We can make it," I said. "Let's go."

"You first," suggested John.

We loaded the cars, moved mine down to streamside, and that's where we were when Jeffrey climbed up the bank, ready to take pictures. Marion eased into the front seat beside me and made a face at him. "I trust you, Ed," she said. "Let's go."

I put it in gear.

Now. Do you need to know what happened? How — or if — we made it across? Does it specifically matter whether or not our feet got wet, or if our cars got stuck, or that Lucinda Hills is now a college graduate herself? That her father and I still go walking in rivers, sometimes together? No. I don't think so. I think it only matters that we were there. And that it was then.

Things were rising. Unseen swirls lifted beneath us and we were gone with them, sliding downhill toward consequences.

• • •

SOME OPEN WATER

WINTER

AT THE BROKEN DAM

Fishing an Icy Glen

WINTER

The medium blue dun hackle spun and straightened, stiff and prim in the blue haze of Ned's pipe smoke.

"There," he said, whip-finishing in an eleven-fingered blur that would have drawn comment at a blackjack table. "Now you do one. It isn't hard."

I blinked. "No... I don't think so. Not yet. You do a couple more while I watch, okay?"

"Yeah. Okay. But you gotta watch closely, now." I could see him bounce a little as he turned back to the bench, reaching for the head cement and humming a Bing Crosby tune.

It was late February and Ned's den was rigged up for fly tying. In fact, the room was more of a workshop than the usual wood-panel and leather arrangement you might expect. Ned's tying materials were in small wooden drawers with brass pulls; tools hung all in reach and sequence, giving a sort of surgical-but-sporty demeanor to the room, and there was a half-finished bamboo rod in sections on the bigger bench by the window. I was out of my element here.

We both knew that, of course, as this was just another session in

Ned's still-fruitless attempt to initiate me to the year-round rituals of the obsessed dry fly fisherman. And, as before, I was failing to get into it.

So when Ned turned back to the Thompson, I turned to his bookshelf.

It was what I expected—Flick, Schwiebert, Darbee, Jorgensen; a couple of Derrydales, the old edition of McLanes's, some leather-bound salmon stuff that I didn't recognize, and one called *How to Fly Fish*.

How to *fly* fish? In Ned's den? You'd have a better chance of finding training wheels in Evel Knievel's garage. I had to check it out; the early days of the Moisie Club could wait for another day.

But there was no revelation here. It was, indeed, just another how-to book for the gentle art initiate, and I decided to give it my standardized test.

I turned to the chapter on dry fly presentation.

As I had hoped, there were pictures here, nice pictures of Catskill-looking streams and exciting pictures of big water on the Yellowstone. There were backlit photographs of tight loops (labeled "good") and open loops ("bad"); there were overhead drawings of downstream bellies creating drag ("very bad") and a pretty picture of a guy in one of those Irish tweed hats deftly mending line upstream ("correct"). Then I turned the page and found a picture of Indian Stream.

Well it didn't *say* it was Indian Stream—you could only see a hundred yards or so of the water—and I knew the guy who wrote this book would never take the trouble to find Indian Stream, but it sure looked like our own little Indian Stream to me.

It looked like the stretch near the old lumbering camp where Becky hooked her first brook trout. The pool there is long, tailing off to a smooth chute before it falls quickly into the big pool formed by No Name Brook.

Becky had waded out to the middle, partly because her backcast was in less trouble out there, and partly because she just wanted to be in the middle of the river. She was still experimenting

WINTER'S ENCRUSTED EDGE

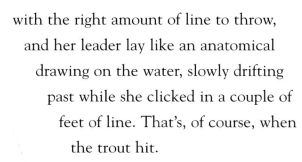

with the right amount of line to throw, and her leader lay like an anatomical drawing on the water, slowly drifting past while she clicked in a couple of feet of line. That's, of course, when the trout hit.

And hit again. And again. Each time spitting out the fly to watch it pop to the surface like an emerger. Becky was madly pulling line to get out the slack, and when she seemed to stop and stare blankly into the water, I shouted encouragement and told her to hurry up.

"How can I?" she shouted back. "The little bugger's *looking* at me."

I could see it all in the picture in Ned's book. Becky standing in the moving water, staring in disbelief at the brook trout swimming in the moving water and staring in disbelief at Becky. Finally she threw up her hands, still holding the rod, and the movement at last took the slack out of the leader, riffling the fly, and causing the trout to take one more time.

The trout on Indian Stream may not be as practiced as a Battenkill brown, but they are very, very wild and they don't often see people. Becky and I have been back, and while the times there have been sometimes funny and sometimes dark, they have become times etched, carved prominently in a place where a simple photograph in an even simpler book can take me there wholly, leaving only an out-of-contact shell behind, like the blanked-out volunteer in a night club hypnotist's show.

Books always do that to me, and it seems to happen more regularly in instruction books. Maybe it's because I still read them a lot.

Not that I'm still trying to learn the nail knot, but in the winter, when Ned and his club members are tying and wrapping, I'll be flipping through a Joe Brooks chapter on trout leaders or a Ray

Ovington discussion of how to approach a mid-stream rock. And when the book lists the taper lengths to tie for a Number 14 wet fly, I'll be tying on a Parmachenee Belle with the wind at my back on Eagle Lake; when the drawing shows a trout silhouette with little arrows around it to describe a back eddy, I'll be trying to reach just upstream of Trafton Rock with a stretched double haul on a June afternoon; when—

"Okay. Your turn now." Ned has turned around and spots the book. "Yeah. I've got to send that back. Forgot to send in the rejection to the book club. You'd think they'd wise up and stop this endless how-to stuff, wouldn't you?"

Quietly I can feel myself rushing and shrinking back into the room. Into Ned's house, here in the winter.

"Oh, I don't know, Ned." Just a mumble. "I'm not so sure."

•　•　•

THE LAST OF THE ICE

FLOATING THE RIVER

ALASKA

The best time to go fishing is when you can't, when winter's cold has seeped as deeply into your own blood as it has into the veins of the deep-hunkered fish themselves, chilling from both of you the quickness that won't reappear until the distant heated rushes of spring. In those shortened, darker days, as the surface of the water itself hardens and seals you from each other, the only thing left is to dream. And to plan.

And if you're going to plan, you ought to plan big. You ought to plan on Alaska.

Remember your early days as a fly fisherman? Do you recall the mystery, the anticipation of not knowing much each time you threw a line onto dark water over unknown fish? What kind are they? Where are they? How big are they? What'll I do if one bites?

Slam! Splash! Pull! Uh oh. Oh geez. Now what?

Hard to beat the excitement, wasn't it? Wouldn't it be cool to be there again? To be a wide-eyed kid on the stream with a rod in your hand and someone to tell you what to do next? With nothing to do

A Heavy Fish

but fish all day, catch 'em till your arm hurts, eat like a hog and fall like a stump into your rack at night? And, hey yeah, maybe there's a grizzly bear out there somewhere. Yeah, right outside your window maybe. No no, wait— Outside your *tent!*

Hi. Welcome to Alaska. Did you bring a fly rod?

Your first trip to an Alaskan fishing lodge is a lot like going off to summer camp, and if you're headed upriver to a tent-based operation, it's even more so. Counselors will meet you when you get off the plane, people will take care of your duffel bags, and someone will check your name off on a clip-board. You'll board the bus (actually a floatplane, but in Alaska that is a bus) with your soon-to-be new friends and you'll be led off to a strange, excit-ing, and slightly intimidating new place.

When you get there, you'll be assigned a tent mate if you didn't sign up with a pal from home, and one of the counselors will check to make sure you brought all the right equipment. They'll show you where the bathroom is and tell you what time to be ready for supper. You might even get a new hat to wear.

On the first morning there will be an orienta-tion meeting and then you'll divide up into preassigned smaller groups and the day's activities will begin. Most of you will be new kids, but there will probably be a veteran or two in camp, already making wisecracks with the counselors on the way out to the boats.

And then you'll go fishing. Some of the unsmoothed newness of it all will now rub down toward familiar edges. You'll have your best fly rod in your hand, with the cork darkened from all those prior casts, and as you step into the current, the water streaming around your old waders will feel just exactly like it does at home. Across the river will be a foam-edged seam that begs a cast, and you'll make one. But it won't be the same. There will be one huge difference:

You won't be casting to a fish. You'll be

casting to a species.

In coastal streams a thousand fresh silver salmon may have come into the river overnight, surging past the spent carcasses of who knows how many earlier sockeyes and kings and jockeying for position among the sea-run Dolly Varden that arrived earlier to crowd it up with the native arctic grayling and rainbow trout that never left. When you step into the Goodnews or the Togiak or the Kanektok, your fly won't be directed toward a known holding lie for a specific fish any more than a Central Park breadcrumb can have one individual pigeon's name on it. Just toss it out and watch the rush.

And there, in the hungered, heedless surge of its wild, quick-feeding fish lies both the beauty and the curse of Alaskan fishing. For if there is nothing so priceless as a wild rainbow trout that has never seen a fly, there is very little that's easier than getting it to eat one. In Alaska, if you can cast all of the leader and a little of the fly line, and if at the end of that leader is a fly your guide has suggested,

you will catch fish. And you will catch them as well as any one else on the trip. For experienced fly fishermen, and for old-line Atlantic salmon anglers in particular, this can be a humbling combination.

The first year that Becky and I went to Alaska, it was to a tent camp in the Togiak Wilderness. In September. The primary fish in the river we camped on, at that time of year, was the silver salmon. Down in the tide-affected estuaries where we stood on gravel bars to cast, the holding pools were alive with very fresh fish, most of them as long as your arm.

The preferred pattern in that water is a traditional Alaskan tie called a "flash fly." It's exactly that: a pinch of shiny Christmas tinsel wound with a splash of red hackle onto a large hook, usually a 1/0. To say that it flashes brightly in the water is to allow that Las Vegas has street lights. You can get these flies from the catalogs before you go, but most of the tent camps have them there, pre-tied in wholesale lots by sub-equatorial piece workers who

Alaskan Gravel Bar

KING SALMON

might or might not have bothered spinning any hair or feathers into the things. Everyone in Alaska knows how to spell "utilitarian."

In our group that first year were several first-time fly fishers who dutifully tied on tinsel flies and immediately caught fish. Becky and I weren't first-time fly fishers but we did, well, follow the leader.

Why not? We tied on tinsel flies and immediately caught fish. Bright, strong silver salmon with sea lice still on them and the open ocean in their eyes.

One man in the group, a retired president of a large manufacturing company, slipped away from the rest of us. I watched as he waded into another pool, well downstream, and began to cast. Long, graceful loops and dragless drifts, down and across, followed by effortless pickups, a step downstream and the same thing all over again. His fly covered the water like a science museum pendulum leaving symmetrical patterns in a smoothed sandbox. At the top of the pool he stopped, reached into his old vest, pulled out a Wheatley fly box and changed patterns. He then moved back to the top of the pool and covered it again. It was elegant, and it was beautiful to watch. He never hooked a fish.

After an hour or so, I wandered down to talk to him. We'll call him Walter.

"How did you do?" he asked affably.

"Caught a few," I answered. "And you?"

"Not yet," he said. "Beautiful place, though, isn't it?"

"Unbelievable," I answered.

Across the river from us, the foothills of the Ahklun Mountains rose from the coastal plain, treeless and tundra-blanketed in bright, mixed gradations of autumn reds, yellows and fading green intersticed with hardened croppings of glacial rock. Low clouds hung in the valleys and there was a distant, hollow silence above the river gurgle that you could have felt even over a turned up Walkman. No one here, however, was wearing a headset.

Walter took out his fly box to select his next attempt. Inside the box, arranged by size and color variance were dozens of perfectly tied Atlantic salmon flies. These came from no one's catalog.

"Your ties?" I asked.

"Just something I do in the winter," answered Walter. "I'm not sure they'll work here, but I thought it would be fun to try." He picked a Bomber, sparsely brown and elegantly trimmed.

"I'm not sure these silvers will take on the top," I offered.

Walter tied it on. "No. Probably not," he said, "but I thought I'd try anyway." He stepped back to the pool. Walter wasn't unfriendly, but it was clear that he wanted to be alone. I moved back to where I'd been fishing. In a few minutes I was hooked up again.

For two days, Walter fished that way, picking sequentially from his fly box, patiently working through all those hours of tying, and methodically covering water that was at a remove from the rest of us. Finally, he hooked one. As he played it, he caught my eye and waved for me to come over.

The fish was still strong, his rod deeply bent.

"I wonder if you would get my camera," he asked.

"It's in the bag behind me."

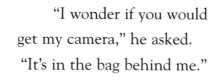

I did, and when he had the played-out fish in the shallows, I took his picture with it. In the corner of the bright salmon's mouth was a Blue Charm, about a size six.

"I did have to get a bit gaudy with them finally," he said as he released the salmon and took his camera back. "But I just wanted to catch one on my own tie. Thanks for taking the picture."

"No problem," I said. "Nice fish." I turned to leave him alone again.

"Say," he said. "You don't have one of those flash flies to spare, do you?"

For the rest of the trip, Walter's Wheatley box stayed in his tent. Taking turns in the good pools with the rest of us, he heaved tinsel and cranked in salmon, whooping it up on the stream and in the cook tent at night, falling into the Alaskan rhythm as creaselessly as he had worked the water the first time I'd watched him.

• • •

*F*ishing in Alaska means, almost universally, fishing with other people. Unless you live there it's almost impossible to arrange a solo trip, and even if you did, you would still have to hire a float plane to get you back to the kind of water you'd really want to be alone on, and to get away from the others with the same idea. But that, too, might not work, as Becky and I learned.

Flowing into 90-mile-long Iliamna Lake is a not-quite-nameless creek where every year the biggest inland rainbow trout in Alaska congregate, holding in the deeper lake water until something — water temperature, daylight length, piscine karma, boredom — draws them closer to the little creek's mouth. There they school like steelhead returning from the sea, and for a couple of weeks, in small pods and at random times, they swim up into the creek itself to spawn.

For years Becky and I had heard of this place, and when Ted Gerken offered to take us there we showed up at pre-dawn breakfast in his Iliaska Lodge with our waders already on. He batted neither eye.

"Good thinking," he said. "Got to get there early if we want a spot."

The mouth of the creek is altered every year as the ice-choked spring runoff forces its way through the natural gravel beach there, but it isn't usually more than a long flycast across. And the long casters do arrive, flying in daily from the many fishing lodges in the area to take turns in the prime spots and politely giving way to anyone lucky enough to hook one of the swimming trophies.

Ted landed his float plane on the lake before the sun was fully up, knowing what Becky and I would soon learn: that an airshow of Cessnas, Beavers and Piper Cubs would appear all morning long, making low passes to count the anglers already there before moving on to another place. As we built a little fire to keep warm and make coffee, we were glad to be the first plane on the beach.

Holding Fast

We weren't, however, the first people there. Someone had made a camp down the gravel bar a hundred or so yards, and there were three tents pitched. The occupants were apparently still sleeping, knowing the other attribute of the place that we were about to learn: that the fishing wouldn't start until mid-morning when the sun warmed the water.

Ted knew this too, of course. He had other guests to deal with, so, as planned, he left us with one of his guides and flew back to the lodge. The guide watched while Becky and I strung up and fished anyway. We were in the very heart of Alaska's designated trophy rainbow water and we weren't going to be here tomorrow. So we cast. And cast. And cast.

About two hours later I hooked one. The fish took the fly in the strong current right at the creek's mouth, putting a huge bend in my nine-foot fly rod and then I just held on as the big rainbow ran like a bonefish for the deep water of the lake. No trout had ever done anything like that to me, and it took me a long time to recover all the backing that had gone out on that run. As the fish tired I brought it near the gravel beach and the guide waded out and very carefully handled the fish, cradling it in the water and not lifting as he gently pulled out the barbless hook. The rainbow was as bright-metallic and hard as a steelhead, almost two feet long and shaped like a football. I'd never seen anything like it.

"God," I said. "Look at it."

"About seven pounds," said the guide. "Want to measure it?"

"No, let's just get it back." I traded my rod for the fish and, keeping the trout just under the surface and cradled in both hands, I led it over to the current of the creek and held it there for a long time while the oxygen-rich flow washed through its gills. My hands got numb, then aching, from the cold before the fish calmly rejuvenated and swam slowly away from me. I stood stiffly up and shuffled toward Becky and the guide. A fisherman was with them, one of the guys from the tents, sipping coffee.

"Nice release," he said. "You've done that before."

"Yeah," I answered, "but never on one like that."

"Saw the first run," he said. "For a minute there I thought you had one of the good ones."

Becky and I just looked at him.

"There's plenty over ten out there," he said. "I got a fifteen yesterday. Want to see it?"

"See it with what, scuba?" I asked.

"No, I killed it," he said. "Come on over to camp. I'll show you."

He turned and started away. We followed.

Over by his tent the guy carefully unwrapped a trout as long as my leg. It was packed in salt, wrapped in foil, kept in a cooler. The color was gone.

"Been coming here for ten years," the guy said. "The same week every year, and I've never killed one before. This one's going on my wall. I don't expect to get one better."

He looked at me and Becky, and I could see he was gauging our reaction.

"Look," he went on. "I thought long and hard about it all winter, but I finally decided that if I did get a good one this time, I'd have it mounted. It's only one fish in ten years. I've let hundreds go, dozens of big ones. It's the only one I've ever killed."

He looked even harder, but I doubt he learned much from our faces. I wasn't so sure myself how I felt, but I did know one thing for certain: If the guy had caught and released that many fish at this creek, then the dead one he now held was most definitely not the first one he ever killed here. And it probably wasn't the first big one, either.

Multiple studies over many years have shown that even the most cautious trout-handlers will cause a five to ten percent mortality in the fish they release. So I calculated as Becky and I walked away from his camp that this obviously thoughtful angler and his friends had probably, over the ten annual weeks they'd camped and fished here, killed something like a fish a day between them.

And what bothered me most is that in all those starry nights by their driftwood campfires in that gorgeous wilderness, these men had not once savored the wild, delicate flavor of one of its native rainbow trout.

• • •

*C*atch and release is the bedrock of fish-eries conservation, and we all practice it without much analysis. Common sense dictates it, we assume, even where the law doesn't.

Almost all of the Bristol Bay lodges and tent camps in Alaska operate on a modified no-kill policy that's substantially stricter than the state regulations that actually govern the water they fish. It's obviously in their best interests to keep as many fish in the river as possible, and it's not even vaguely practical for their customers to take fresh fish home with them. The guides all carry stout pliers for pinching down your barbs, and many of them won't even let you touch your own caught rainbow until they've personally de-hooked and revived it to the point where they think the fish can stand up to your amateur fumbling. This may be the fish of your lifetime, but the guide may be handling it for the third time this month. It can get pretty personal with them.

On the other hand, these operations are deep in the wilderness, everything has to be flown in by bush plane, and they have to feed the people. Fish, therefore, is going to be on the menu. The ones I've been to handle this quandary in varying ways.

Top-of-the-checkbook lodges simply avoid it altogether, flying in frozen steaks and fresh vegetables often enough to dodge the issue and occasionally serving fresh salmon caught out in the salt water by commercial netters. Most of the others, especially the remote tent camps, have to use locally-caught fish: early-run salmon if the camp is near enough to the estuary to have access to fresh ones, or big northern pike in the upriver locations. None of them ever serve rainbow trout. To the guests anyway.

The usual dinner-catching procedure is to let the apprentice "guides" (whose real jobs are to sweep tents and clean toilets) go out after the sports have left for the day and heave spinning lures into the river, quickly catching whatever is needed for the upcoming evening meal. The fish are cleaned, cooled and kitchened long before the flycasters return from their long day of carefully-monitored releases. The post-cocktail question of where tonight's broiled fillet came from doesn't usually come up, but if it does the lodge outfitter usually tells the straight story. After all, it's just enough for dinner.

Limit your kill, don't kill your limit. Right?

Some of the long-time guides can get pretty far removed, however, from their early days as latrine-swabbers and fish-getters. If they ever had them. One year in a camp Becky and I had been to several times, there was a new guide from New Zealand, an excellent fly fisherman and trout-spotter on a sort of sabbatical, guiding in Alaska. He'd never been there before, but was well-known in his country. Call him Fishmael.

We were miles upriver from camp, late in the afternoon, when the the base camp radioed to him that there had been a snafu and no one had obtained the needed fish for tonight's dinner. There were twelve hungry guests and a staff of eight.

"No problem," I told him. "Tell them we'll bring in a bunch of Dolly Vardens."

In truth it was no problem. The Dollies were everywhere, flashing in the thigh-deep current, and all you had to do was put on a metallic fly of some kind and you could get one on nearly every cast. We'd just spent half the day avoiding them by using dark flies and egg patterns, trying to get the rainbows mixed in with them. I gave Fishmael my spare rod and we went after them. This was a treat.

Fishing for food because we had to. The real thing.

We each hooked a few little ones and threw them back before Fishmael brought in a good one, maybe four pounds. I flashed him a thumbs-up and watched as he fumbled with the writhing fish. They are hard to hold.

"What do I do now?" he called.

"Kill it," I said.

He nodded and wrestled with the slippery fish. They never stop twisting. He tried to re-grip it, barely holding on, and then he looked at me quizzically.

"How do you do that?" he asked.

• • •

THE LONG CAST

The food chain in and around an Alaskan river is a lot like that in the Gulf Stream: It's in constant tension and you're not technically at the top of it. But in practice, of course, you're not much of a part of it either. The brown bears aren't about to walk away from their salmon cafeteria to try to run you down, especially now that guides and park rangers have for several bruin generations been practicing applied Darwinism with shotguns and large-bore handguns. You'll probably be consumed by the beauty of an Alaskan river and its residents, but you won't get eaten there.

This is not to detract, however, from the generalized ferocity that is never far beneath the surface of those gently burbling streams. Literally. Take a conceptual leap into the Gulf Stream for a minute and imagine yourself covered with and reeking of shark attractant. Now start floundering and splashing helplessly on the surface. Can you sense it? Can't you just feel something coming?

Something huge and underwater and accelerating toward you...?

You're a deer-hair mouse dropped next to a grass bank on the Mulchatna River.

Rainbow trout have teeth, and in Alaska they use them. A lot. Summer is short, winter is long, and bite-sized protein doesn't float free for very long. Under every cutbank and deadfall will be a stationed rainbow, and it won't be looking for a Black Gnat on a 7X tippet. In most places it won't be looking for any sort of dry fly, and in the few rivers where the fish do take dries, they take them in June and July only. Try it in September and you literally will never get a rise. On the other hand, the coastal plain is home to millions of lemmings and other small furry critters that fall continually into rivers. And into trout mouths.

The first time I tried mousing on an Alaskan stream, I did it from a high bank, about six feet above the water on a long, gradual bend in the river. The others in our boat had stayed on a good gravel bank to cast streamers to a pool full of salmon, and I had decided to take a little upstream hike. The sky was cloudless and the midday sun warm.

From up on the grassy bank, looking through my polaroids, I could see every rock on the bottom of the river. There weren't any salmon here in the relatively fast water between holding pools, and I couldn't make out any other fish, either. Dolly Varden show themselves by "flashing" in the current as they roll and tip sideways, letting the sun glint on their very smooth, shiny flanks. Grayling are active in the flow, moving often and leaving shadows on the bottom. There weren't, according to the guide, likely to be rainbows in this stretch. It was lovely water nonetheless, and I stopped to sit down.

Since I was on the outside of this long curve in the river, the flow had cut a deep channel along my side of the river, showing as a narrow green-to-blue crescent carved out against the bank for a hundred or more yards downstream from where I sat. It was too deep to see the bottom, and I just

knew there had to be fish in it. I also knew that if I cast to them from up here, they'd certainly see the line and the waving rod in the air above them. On a whim, I took out my one deer hair mouse.

I had had the mouse for a long time, tucked in among my smallmouth bass bugs; I hadn't tied it on in years. It was a bushy, wind-resistant thing to cast, and back when I had first got it I wasn't much of a fly caster. After a few marginally successful tries in Maine, I had let it stay in the box. Exciting as it was when a bass hit it, the tradeoff had been hours of sloppy, arm-wrenching casting. I'm not really sure why I brought it to Alaska that first time. Probably something I read.

In any case, here on the Alaskan stream, I did it the easy way. Stripping most of the fly line off the reel and onto the grass, I lobbed a short cast down and against the bank, and then I fed line out as the current swiftly took the bobbing little mouse down the channel.

The rainbow came from all the way across the

FISHING CAMP ON THE GOOD NEWS RIVER, ALASKA

STRIKE AT THE BEAVER HOUSE

river. Accelerating like a barracuda on the flats, it streaked across faster than I could actually register what was happening and it hit the mouse like a thrown brick. In an instant the fish was in the air and shaking, then back with a crash and off across the shallows, zipping fly line sideways across the surface with a sizzling sound like ripping paper, pulling the slack through my fingers and snapping the last of it taught against the reel without my having to turn the crank once.

I fought the fish for a long time, working it downstream to where I could get in the water and bring it close enough to play out and let go. The rainbow slowly swam away. I looked around.

There wasn't another person in sight. The river was as placid as it had been before the trout struck, the time-ripples of the event gone and dissipated into the wilderness surrounding me as completely as if they had never been stirred in the first place. I carefully clipped off the mouse and put it in my fly box.

Far across the tundra valley the hills rose toward Bristol Bay, off to the south. A pair of sandhill cranes wobbled like stick figures with wings against the sky; a raven croaked from somewhere behind me, far away. And in the river where I stood, a pod of a dozen salmon came swimming upstream, steady against the current and ghosting past me with a concentrated indifference that literally filled me with — what can I call it? — an exultant rush of calm, a lifting sense of place, a quiet flood of being alive. And it made me want to cry.

The afternoon air was warm, endless and expanding, the riffled current sussurant by my side, crystal blue and glinting in the low sunlight; I couldn't have told you what day it was. Tucking my fly rod under my arm, I crossed the river and started back upriver toward the others.

• • •

In no other place that I know are the endless rhythms of subarctic seasonality and sea-run spawning so intensely combined as they are in Alaska, where the great flood of each thawing winter meets the swimming surge of whole species regenerating themselves in countless rushing chutes, riffles, gorges, rapids and pools over an expanse of wild country almost devoid of human presence. In this vast setting it's the hook in the water, and not much else, that puts you in contact, and minimally at that. The place doesn't even know you exist. Doesn't even care. And no matter how much you care, it doesn't matter, it comes nowhere near a balance. A fleeting touch is all you'll get.

But it's all you'll need. The angling lessons of Alaska are as simple as they are overwhelming, because they teach you once and for all that it's only the hook that connects you to what you want, and it only matters that you know why, not how, to get that hook to the fish. The niceties of presention and the mastered fluidics of the reach cast may be entry-level requirements to try the sulking mysteries of the Henrys Fork in August, but not on the Nushagak in July. The answers are available to everyone who goes there with a fly rod, novice or expert, wide-eyed kid or really wide-eyed adult. Everyone sees the silver; each can be touched by the rainbow.

Alaska, more than any other fishing I know, and much like life itself, rewards you best when you finally recognize that your part in it is important only to you, and occasionally to those around you. The ecosystem itself is completely indifferent — at least in the short run of, say, your lifetime — and the fish that present themselves to you there reward not your attained skill as an angler but the simple fact that you have presented yourself to them.

• • •

SPRING

POLING UPRIVER

SILVERY MORNING

SPRING

We're waist deep in the Big Muddy
And the big fool says to push on.
                                    —*Pete Seeger*

The first thing I ever bought with a credit card was a canoe. The card arrived in the mail on a spring Thursday in 1972 and by Saturday the canoe was on top of my old Chevy and the credit card in a desk drawer, already maxed out with that one purchase. I can't recall which collection agency finally took the card away, but the canoe lasted until just last year, its mahogany ribs and oft-recaned seats finally giving it up and easing into the irrecoverable sag of old boats everywhere.

I kept the canoe, a 13-foot Merrimack, green fiberglass hand-laid over wooden ribs, for years after it was beyond repair, letting it sit inverted on sawhorses in the back yard, hanging onto the thing the way you keep any talisman that really does work.

Even in the deep of winter the little green canoe could take me away as well, or better, than albums of photographs to the places that we had been together. I'd go out at night, layered in wool and trudging behind the dog for a snow-silenced walk under brittle starlight, and there would be the familiar dark shape, double-ended, calling

WORKING THE SHORELINE

silently to me in codes of woodsmoke, waterproof duffels, quick-running northern rivers and fly line stripped and ready on canoe ribs between my feet.

In the spring, however, as the New England snow melted around it and the days lengthened toward ice-out, the canoe would speak almost out loud to me.

Come on, it would whisper. *It's time. It's time to go. It's time to glide.*

. . .

Fly fishing from a canoe on quiet water may be the single most predatory way to approach a feeding fish. On flat water, with the wind light enough to let you see a rising fish, you can ease into casting position as silently as the trout or bass approached whatever it was that it just attacked. Drifting in like a cloud shadow, you'll be relaxed and comfortable, literally sitting down in a giant stripping basket, and your cast can be as long — or as short — as you want it to be.

And, of course, you don't have to wait for a sighted feeder. Letting the wind push you slowly down the rocky shore of a New Hampshire lake as you drop little yellow popping bugs an inch or two from dry land before scuttling them out over deeper water is an almost embarrasingly better smallmouth technique than lobbing crankbaits anywhere near the same fish. I know this with some certainty, as I've been running a controlled experiment for several years now.

My son Will has been a serious fisherman since he could climb unaided into a canoe. He's one of those luck-dusted fishermen who always — and I mean always — catches something. You know people like this. A researcher with a closet full of tackle and a glib tongue may someday juke his way into a study grant on the causes of this unfair distribution of the sporting chance, but until that gets published the rest of us will simply have to sit in the other end of the canoe and spit invective at the annoying fish gods. Silently, of course, if the fortune-mantled caster in the bow is your own twelve-year-old son.

In any case, Will's tool of choice has been the ultralight spinning rod with a Panther Martin at the wet end. For the first few years that he and I canoed the edges of Naughname Pond, his overall technique, while good once the lure hit the water, was lacking in consistency of control. We got good at retrieving Panther Martins from overhanging white pines and I spent a fair amount of each outing picking snarls from his open-faced reel. It was a full-time job keeping his gear functional and, in short, I never even brought a rod for myself. Will had a voice-activated canoe-control device in the stern seat, and I got to watch him catch fish.

But in the last two years, Will has become self-sufficient. He's accurate with his casts, and knows how to prevent line twist. He changes lures with pit-crew efficiency, and he always has had the instinctive good sense to keep casting. He used to catch a lot of fish; now he catches a *lot* of fish. And now that he's on his own up front in the canoe, I've started bringing along my seven-weight and bass bugs. These days I match him about cast for cast, fly-rod bug against everything in his tackle box, and it's not even a contest.

"Hey, Dad," he said about half way through last summer. "I want to learn how to fly fish."

• • •

Sitting in the stern seat of a canoe gives you a sort of OmniMax theater view of the world around you. The canoe itself points straight away no matter how or where you steer it, and your whole field of view swings past the fixed reference jutting 12 or 15 feet out from where you sit. If someone is sitting in the canoe's bow then the big-screen theater image is heightened, as if the only other guy who bought a

CASTING

MORNING MIST

ticket decided to sit right in front of you, two rows away. Waving a fly rod.

When you are in the bow, however, the obverse holds. You seem to be perched on a dime-thin platform that tips precariously side to side as you are propelled from behind through an unstable universe that is all too three-dimensional. The water is literally at your feet, all around, and if you lean out over the bow you can skim like a swallow over the surface and cast any time you want to anything in range. It's absolutely the better end of the deal, almost surreal if your partner knows how to paddle, but one you rarely get if the canoe belongs to you. The stern seat's for the skipper. But not always.

When I had had that first canoe for two or three years, and after I had found one particular lake to fish from it, I got a Saturday morning call from a neighbor named, say, Vronsky. I had only known him for a short time, but we had the outdoors in common and I liked the guy. Vronsky said he wanted to go fishing right away and could we

take my canoe. It was a warm spring morning and I had a full day of chores to do. Vronsky was insistent.

When we got to the lake, Vronsky said he wanted to paddle from the stern. I could do most of the fishing, he said. Fine, I agreed. We rigged fly rods and pushed off.

The lake is in a state park in Massachusetts, a former estate that doesn't get much publicity in the tourism brochures. The water is no good for swimming or any kind of boating besides what we were doing — paddling through acres of duck weed and lily pads, gliding behind small islands and dropping bass bugs into small pockets of open water.

With Vronsky in the stern, we covered a lot of water. We were both in our 20's and he had played college football; the guy was still in shape and a strong paddler, and my little canoe moved around the lake at a clip that it hadn't done before. He would paddle us fast from one likely hole to the next; I'd drop a cast or two there, and then he would move us off again. He paddled too hard, and I didn't

really like the pace he was setting. I don't think we spoke a word. After about an hour of strikeless casting and hard paddling, I finally got a hit.

The bass dove immediately into the thick mat of vegetation that clogs 70 percent of the water there, and I steadily dredged it back to the canoe, lifted off the weeds and released the fish, a nice largemouth, about two pounds. Vronsky sat there for a minute without picking up either his fly rod or the paddle. He was looking away.

"Got a minute?" he asked.

"The rest of the day," I answered.

Her name was Karen, he told me, and he had kept seeing her long after he'd been married. Off and on, even after Vronsky's kids were born. About a year ago he had told Karen he wasn't going to see her anymore. She was obsessive, he said, and complex; he had known her since high school, way before he had met his wife, who knew all about her.

"All about her?" I tried to delicately put it. For a long time he didn't answer.

"Karen's brother called me this morning," he said quietly. "Just before I called you. She killed herself. Pills. Didn't leave a note. I had to get away, so I called you. Sorry."

Vronsky fiddled with a new fly, didn't say anything more about it. When I realized that his story was over, I stripped out some line and made a sloppy cast toward an opening that was outside my range. I tried to pick up and got tangled in the weeds. He watched as I pulled in the bass bug, cleared it and tried another cast. It slopped off to the right, tangled again.

"How did you find this place?" asked Vronsky.

"Just poking around," I said as I picked the salad from my fly. "It looks so good, but I haven't landed a good one yet."

He rolled out his line, lifted cleanly and shot a long, smooth cast that landed perfectly in the place I couldn't quite get to. The bug sat there as its ripples disappeared into the thick green plants all around it.

"Too many weeds," he said. "There's no way to get back."

• • •

Most of my time in a canoe has been spent alone. Silence is so essential a component of canoe fishing that going solo truly is the only proper way to do it. Cut down to its basics — seamless hull, ash paddle, fly rod and you — the game is far simpler than most river wading. No cleated waders, multi-tool-infested vests, polarized glasses; no calculus of hydrodynamics and back eddy effects on fly presentation; no downstream disruption from up-trodden silt. Flats fishing in cutoff shorts with a couple of spare flies in your pocket is the closest wading can come to the pure simplicity of a lone caster in a clean canoe.

For a good number of years, back when I lived closer to bass ponds than to the trout water that's

BASS FISHING ON THE CURRENT RIVER, MISSOURI

nearby these days, I used to drive to a small natural pond that had no houses on it. Largemouth, pickerel, black crappie and several varieties of sunfish were there in abundance. Within an hour of getting home from work on a summer evening, I could be on that water in my canoe and I did it a couple of nights a week. There was a large, well-publicized lake with a public boat ramp just a mile or so away; I never saw another fisherman on my little water.

Most of the time I harassed the sunfish with a five-weight trout outfit. They were dependable surface-strikers even in the heat of August, and I threw Wulffs and humpies at them instead of the more textbook foam poppers. Occasionally a slashing pickerel would show itself and I'd change to a streamer, usually not in time. Other evenings I'd bring along a heavier rig and throw deer-hair bugs at places where bass ought to be, but nine hits out of ten would be the crappie, named, I decided, after the quality of the fight if you hooked one.

On about my third or fourth trip to the pond,

as I cruised a deep little inlet, I saw another canoe, up on the shore and chained to an old pine tree. I beached mine and investigated. There was a path back in the woods that wound all the way back to the road near where I always parked. The canoe was old aluminum and the chain rusted, but the padlock was new. Not a beer can, cigarette butt or discarded snelled-hook package to be seen. The owner was, I decided, okay. Somebody to talk to when he and I crossed wakes some evening.

In four years of fishing the pond, I never saw him.

His canoe was always there, though, waiting. It got to where I'd make a point of paddling over to the inlet each time I fished the pond. I'd look at the canoe, chained in the same way to the same tree, and then I'd move on to shallower water and begin casting.

The last summer I lived nearby, there was a drought and the level of the pond had dropped six or eight inches by mid July. It had been several weeks since I'd made it to the pond, and the water level surprised me. The usual launching spot had turned into a nasty little mud drag, and most of the my sunnie hot spots were only inches deep. I set out to find new structure. As always, I had the place to myself.

Most of the holding water, of course, was simply a few yards out from where it had been previously. All I had to do was drift closer to the center of the pond and cast my usual distance, and there were the fish. I caught some sunfish, then decided to head up to the deeper inlet where the canoe would be chained to the pine tree.

As I quietly paddled around the bend in the shoreline, turning to go up into the inlet, I saw a log sticking about two inches out of the water, right in the middle of the inlet. An old tree stump, it had clearly been there for years, completely submerged and hidden in the dark, tannic water until this year's drought revealed it to me. I stopped the canoe's forward slide and tied on a deer hair moth.

One cast did it. The moth barely touched the surface a foot from the log and the water exploded. One second later the bass was in the air, throwing showers and showing red gills before *galunk*-ing back into the water and taking out line. It took me ten minutes on the little trout rod to get the fish to lay over on its side and come in. A 19-inch largemouth, so big and such a surprise that I almost kept it to show Becky. But as I held it in the water, I decided not to. I now knew where this fish lived, even if the water level went back up and obscured the log it called home. It was right here in the deep inlet where the canoe was chained. I could find it again.

So I decided instead to show the fish, ceremoniously and in his absentia, to my unknown fishing friend, the owner of the old aluminum canoe. I lifted the big bass and turned toward the pine tree.

The canoe was gone.

• • •

CASTING TO THE RISE

ADIRONDACK LAKE FISHERMAN

When my friend Sarge Collier turned one of those birthday years that ends in a zero, his wife Betsy called me a month or so in advance and said she was throwing a surprise party for him. My job, she said, was to keep Sarge out of the house for the entire day, dawn to dark. And it had to be fail-safe.

"Keep him out of here until seven," she said. "I don't want to see him a minute before then."

"Not a problem," I said. "I'll take him fishing."

Coolly waiting until a week or so before the party, I called Sarge and asked if he wanted to go up to New Hampshire for brook trout the following Saturday. "We can go in my Jeep," I offered.

"Sounds good," he said. "I'll check with Bets to see if anything else is on tap." The surprise was, apparently, still that.

Two days before the party my Jeep broke down, so we ended up taking Sarge's old Land Cruiser, a bare-bones veteran that should have long previous been reassigned to short-haul farm duty. Chugging up Interstate 93 at 40 miles an hour with the butterfly vents opened full to force the monoxide back out through the rust-perforated tailgate, I decided that we weren't going to make it as far north as had been my original plan.

"What do you know about the Sugar River?" I shouted to Sarge.

"I've got a better idea," he said. "There's a little stream near one of my grouse coverts in Sunapee that I've always wanted to try. What do you think?"

"We're there," I said.

An hour later we were off the macadam and onto a dirt road that wound through deep woods and an occasional open hay field. The valley we were in had a nice brook running through it, and Sarge was driving us up toward the shaded headwaters where the water would stay all-day cool. Across one of the fields were alders and a couple of old apple trees.

"That the covert over there?" I asked.

"Nice try," he said. "We went by it a half hour ago. It's not even on this road."

I noted the spot. This was the covert, all right.

It was almost noon by the time we parked the Land Cruiser and strung up. Sarge had been right: this was a small stream worth trying. Classic native brook trout water, you could step across it most places, but there were deeper pockets and cut banks that looked very promising. Sarge tied on a Royal Coachman and dropped it behind a bowling-ball-sized midstream rock. *Ploop!* An instant tiny strike from a four-inch brookie. He turned and grinned.

"I love this stuff," he said.

We separated. Sarge moved upstream and I hiked a quarter mile down so I could work slowly up behind him with enough time to rest the water that he would fish ahead of me. That first quarter-mile, though, would be all mine.

And it was a blast. An elk-hair caddis worked even better than the attractor Coachman. The fish were all small, in the four to six inch range, but they were wild trout and beautiful in the hand as I released them. And every now and then one of them would come fully out of the water to take the little caddis from above, on the way back down. Orvis fish, we called them when they did that.

After a couple of hours, I decided to speed up and find Sarge. A half-mile upstream I found him, on his knees and bent over, concentrating.

"Get down," he hissed as I came closer. "This is a good one."

I stepped behind a white pine to watch. In a billiard-table-sized pool in front of Sarge there were three or four fish rising. One of them did throw more water than I had seen all day.

"He's already seen the Coachman," said Sarge.

"Caddis'll work," I said.

Sarge tied one on and dropped it at the head of the little pool, right under a six-inch waterfall. The fly drifted a foot and the trout took it.

"That's him!" shouted Sarge. The brookie thrashed all over his home pool, then sped out and downstream.

"Going to play him from the reel?" I asked.

"Don't laugh," said Sarge. "This is a hog fish."

I knew it was. Rich with bright little roseates on top of that unclassifiable mix of blue, black and purple that mantles only wild brook trout, with its ivory-edged pectoral fins and bright onyx eyes, this was as stunningly gorgeous as an eight-inch creature gets. In New England anyway.

"This is spectacular," waxed Sarge. "We can fish here till dark."

It was a two-hour drive at the speed limit back to Sarge and Betsy's house. Three minimum in the Toyota beater. I thought about the impending houseful of party guests.

"I've got to be back before that," I said.

Sarge looked at me like I'd just spat in church. "For what?" he said. "What could be better than this?" What could I say? For one thing, he was right. He tied on a fresh elk hair caddis and moved upstream.

We got to Sarge's surprise party three hours late. Some of his friends had already left, and Betsy was beside herself. "How could you do this?" she ranted at me. "I trusted you. Look what you've done." She even called me an asshole. This from a woman who goes regularly to church and really doesn't swear.

Sarge looked at me and shrugged. A silent apology. For the last two hours on the stream, I hadn't even fished. I'd spent the whole time following him, saying it really was time to go and watching him catch more of those wild little brook trout. Toward the end he had to use some of my flies, as his had been all chewed up. A glorious fishing day under every other circumstance but this one.

Even counting this one, I told myself as I lingered in a corner catching daggers from Betsy and a couple of her friends who had spent the day setting up the party.

As I downed my second quick drink, a pariah standing alone, one of Sarge's friends came over. I knew the guy fairly well; he wasn't a fisherman.

"So," he said. "Was it worth it? Good fishing?"

"Great, actually," I answered.

"Got some big ones, huh?"

"Oh yeah," I said. "Sarge got an eight-incher."

The guy laughed, then looked at me. "You're serious," he said.

I nodded. Across the room, Sarge was in a group of his pals, laughing. The guy looked over at him, then back at me.

"Betsy was right," he said.

• • •

SUMMER

THE MOMENT

LATE SUMMER ON THE STREAM

SUMMER

It launch'd forth filament, filament, filament out of itself,
Ever unreeling them, ever tirelessly speeding them.
—*Walt Whitman*

One of the great disappointments of fly fishing is that it isn't better in the summertime. Or, to make the ancient but accurate distinction, it's a shame that the catching isn't better. The fishing, of course, is just fine.

In the long center of summer the days are endless, the evenings warm and the biting bugs on the wane. Your legs never ache from the deep creep of cold through your waders, and you've been casting for enough weeks now that your loops have tightened and your drifts don't drag. Much. Hatches now come off all day long and into the bat-wing hours and half the people you're supposed to deal with at work are on vacation. Time is your friend.

But where are the fish? Why haven't they cycled into this good thing? If they're cold-blooded, how come they don't heat up in the sunshine like you do? If a February trout is sluggish and bottom-hugging, why doesn't an August rainbow torpedo across the river and launch into the shimmering air every time you even hint "grasshopper" to him?

And why, most of all, do they have to eat only those tiny,

67

annoying little specks that can't be imitated and really ought to be delivered on 15X tippets?

I was watching television the other day and saw an ad for one of those motorized leaf blowers, a sort of hair dryer on steroids that blasts a stream of forced air wherever you point it, and just as I hit the remote to escape the nightmare of being in a life where you actually might want one of those things, it occured to me what an awesome fly-delivery system it would make. You could spool gossamer line on an open-faced reel under the bazooka part of the contraption and blow microscopic flies to every lie in the Millionaire's Pool from the parking lot. You could take dropper-fly technology to the next logical level, webbing a few dozen size 28 Tricos into a cannon-net setup that wouldn't try to match a hatch, it would *be* one. You could stride down to the river like Schwarzenegger in a bass-master video: Ignition. *Whoosh!* Yeeh-hah! Reel 'em in, cowboy.

That's the thing about nightmares; they tend to mutate into even better ones. Still, there's something there that, on a reduced scale, just might . . .

Midsummer fly fishing. It can make you nuts. The cure, of course, is to get out there and do it some more.

• • •

If you wade for any distance along the Au Sable near Grayling, Michigan your fishing day will alternate between secluded forest on the banks around you and fishing in someone's back yard. Quite literally. Do this on a midsummer weekend and you'll be part of any number of barbecues, badminton matches and yard parties along the river. The residents won't even notice you unless you fall down, hook a good one or voice an unusual description to a missed strike. Fishermen on the Au Sable are a constant and natural presence in the water; in that ecosystem fly casting is an unremitting but intrusive component that dwellers both above and below the water have long ago learned to tune out. It's not a river you'd go out of your way to fish in August.

But if you did, you'd catch fish. And you wouldn't have to do it after dark. It's a great river, and it is filled with trout.

The trick is to pick a good place and stay there long enough to see how the fish have adapted to the boats. There are canoe-rental shops all along the Au Sable and they do serious business; flotillas of life-jacketed paddlers in aluminum canoes will come by at staccato intervals and you'll hear them coming long before you see them. Most of them are high school or college kids, and some will offer you a beer as they slide past. Take it. You can then cement an instant reputation with the next frat party that comes along by casually handing the beer to one of them. You might hold back if it's Boy Scouts, unless you want to be part of campfire lore for next century.

Meanwhile, carefully observe how long it takes for the fish to begin rising again after the boats go by. Cast at the appropriate interval and

AFTER THE RAIN

A WILDERNESS TROUT POND

you should be in business. This works here only because there is so much boat traffic that the trout have to begin feeding in canoe wakes or they'd starve. And by not floating away, you can fit into the pattern with them.

If you see a fly caster coming downstream in a canoe, or especially if he's being guided in a traditional Au Sable river boat, then your tactic will be different. Just before the new guy gets in range, toss a couple of sloppy casts out there and put your fish down. That way he won't hook one and, with luck and decent timing, you'll have tricked your fish into thinking the guy in the boat was the source of all that scary dumped fly line.

You think I'm kidding, don't you?

Of course if you want to see the real trout, the five-pound browns and their big sisters, then you'll want to take a nap and string up later, after dark, during the "Michigan Caddis" hatch, the spectacular nightime eruption of the *Hexagenia* mayfly in late June. Or are they now called *Litobrancha?* Who

knows. Why care. They're huge, as long as a kid's thumb, and what you can expect is a feeding trout that thinks a bug this small must be a midge.

Regulars who fish the hatch say the right way is to pick a section of river that has good brown trout hideouts — deep cutbanks, old deadfalls, nasty stuff that dumps canoeists — and memorize it in the daytime. That way, when you're out there at 11:30 PM with a big-hackled fly on a long-shank hook whirring through the night sky near most of your sensory organs, you can be a bit more deliberate. The payoff might be the fish of a lifetime. Or a Stephen King heartstop when you're skulking into position and one of the big guys comes out of the water right behind you.

And the big ones are there, fish that you might hook but will never land. Not, at least, in the snag-cobbled currents of the night river, where a two- pound brown knows exactly which hole to sprint for if something stings its jaw. And where the short underwater flurry will possibly draw the very

LOW WATER ON THE YELLOWSTONE

cold attention of the one you didn't hook, the brown trout that just might decide to eat this one if you tire it enough.

On the Au Sable, like any well-frequented vacation spot, you can hang out in the sunshine with the regular folk, having a good time and dodging traffic, or you can run with the predators and do something a bit riskier at night.

• • •

*M*idsummer is long, and the best way to beat it is to rise above it. In the high country streams of Montana, snowmelt keeps rivers roiled and turbid well into June, and July is considered the early season. The August slowdown is hard to avoid in any major river, but if you don't mind a little hike or can handle a saddle horse then the solution lies scattered across the glaciated plateaus north of Yellowstone Park, in the pristine cutthroat lakes of the Beartooth primitive area and along little gems like the Stillwater and Rosebud rivers that drop out of that country through a carved wilderness of Ponderosa pine and vertical granite, purling into the flatter ranchland valleys with cold, crystal water that just a few miles upstream was 4,000 feet higher. August, in this specific environment, is just about right.

My friend J.O. Hash is a third generation rancher from Red Lodge, Montana, which means that he, like most ranchers these days, has to work a couple of jobs on the side in order to keep his family's T O Bar branding irons in the fire every spring. So for about 20 years now he's had a recreational lease on the sublimely beautiful MacKay Ranch that backs up against the Absaroka-Beartooth Wilderness near the town of Roscoe. Hidden in the tall pines and quaking aspens along Morris Creek and the West Branch of the Rosebud, J.O.'s Black Butte Outfitters has two classically laid out wall tent camps, one for elk hunters in the fall and the other for fly fishermen.

MONTANA SPRING CREEK

Summer in the Rockies is pretty much a John Denver song all the way, with the volume turned up if you're in a tent camp up at 6,000 feet whose only access is by horseback. With a clear stream running through the adjacent meadow and the morning sun catching on the surrounding peaks a full two hours before its warming rays will touch down on the river you're going to have to yourself all afternoon, you won't be able to shut off the mountain music even if you wanted to. Just let it play while you string up a light rod and slip into your waders.

What you'll find when you get out on the little Rosebud is that the trout are remarkably picky feeders for fish that live in such a wild place, and with so short a growing season. You'd think that with only a few months without snowpack they would hammer anything buggy that might float by, but they don't. These rainbows and brookies are not hyper technical like the browns in a Pennsylvania limestone run, but they will want something closer to a natural than your basic Wulff pattern if the insect coming off is smaller and downwing, as it usually is. What results is almost perfect trout fishing for all but the most dogma-driven hatch-matchers.

The West Rosebud is a small river that you can wade across without getting your knees wet in most places, but it does empty a vast wilderness of deep snow. The spring surge of ice chunks, rocks and ripped-up trees has gouged any number of cut-banks and deep holes; there are big fish lurking in the green depths between riffles and they seem to have a preference for those out-of-the-current small backwaters behind larger boulders. There, if you approach quietly and stay patient, you can sometimes see a 14- or 16-inch trout gently poke its snout up and into the scud to take ... something you don't have in your vest. Drop a fly in there anyway; it'll be camouflaged by all that other stuff on the surface, but the rainbow won't miss the drop, no matter how lightly you place it there. Throw an

upstream mend to keep it there. Watch it, watch it. And just before you lose your slack, just before the fly is going to be yanked out of there by a big-bellied downstream drag… twitch the fly. *Ploop!* Lift and tighten. Fish on.

Fighting a wild rainbow trout in a setting like that, with ship's-mast sized Ponderosas across the stream, quaking aspens in a natural grass park on your left, and jagged peaks lifting past the treeline and stretching away toward Idaho up the uninhab-ited valley to the right, all of it exuding a profound silence broken only by moving water and wind whisper, is enough to make you want an immediate out-of-body experience in order to float up and stare at yourself. Is this actually happening to me? Can life get any better?

That's about the point where the fish will break off. And if you've got one of those imagina-tions that sometimes gets physical with you, you're going to land hard enough to get a sore butt.

It's okay. The place looks even better sitting

down, with a bunch of slack fly line trailing down-stream toward Billings. We all need a fresh perspective, and an involuntary one tends to be better medicine. I don't know about you, but that's why I go fishing.

• • •

Summer visitors who stay in their vehicles in Yellowstone Park have always been right on the edge of a better experience than most of them realize, begin-ning with the first bunch who watched Chief Joseph and his Nez Perce tribe skulking through the newly-opened park in 1877 on the run from the the U.S. cavalry. Today every photographer and fisher-man knows that the crowd dissipates exponentially with each step away from the road, but that doesn't mean you have to hike for two days up Slough Creek to connect with something wild.

One year we went to Yellowstone as a family

SUMMERTIME

AFTERNOON ON THE YELLOWSTONE

in full tourist camo: We rented a 30-foot RV in Denver and drove up through Jackson Hole and into the Park via the South Entrance. Parking the rig in a designated lot near Indian Creek, one of the upper tributaries of the Gardner River, we decided it was time to go fishing.

Indian Creek is designated as "children's fishing" and is, I believe, the only water inside Yellowstone Park where you're allowed to keep fish. There were a dozen other RV's planted streamside with us, and I had scant hope of catching anything in the creek, since it ran without bankside obstruction less than 50 yards from the parking lot that, I knew, stayed full all season long. But our son Will was four, and he was ready. In our two-week swing through the American West, where the rest of us would in a day or two be drifting the Madison or backpacking up Cache Creek for cutthroats, Will would, realistically, only have this one day on this one creek to fish in a way that might even faintly work for him. I rigged him up with a tiny spinning rod and plastic bobber, then tied a three-foot leader and Royal Coachman to the bobber. Dry fly fishing for a little guy.

Down at the stream, I told Will to wait a minute while I scanned the current with my Polaroids. No point in driving off any stray fish that might actually be here. I was concentrating hard, looking downstream, when I heard Will laugh behind me. I turned around.

He had a fish on. You don't travel a thousand miles, drive for days before finally putting a fishing rod in a kid's hand, then walk him down to an honest-to-God trout stream and tell him to just sit there.

That night we ate Will's brook trout. Along with the other four he caught before I couldn't stand it any longer and went back to the RV and strung up my fly rod.

I didn't catch any.

• • •

No summer's fishing is complete without a drift boat trip down a major river. It might as well be the Madison and you ought to do it in early July, when the winter runoff is complete, the river will be back in shape and the salmon fly hatch might be on.

Sign up at one of the fly shops in Ennis; they've each got guides and boats on call. What you want is a Montana native with a rodeo championship belt buckle and gnarly hands who drives a rattletrap pickup, spits tobacco and packs a lunch cooler so full that even a guy like him needs two hands to hoist it into his McKenzie boat. There's no point in missing the full Western experience if you're going to spend all day with someone under the big sky.

You'll probably start at the McAtee Bridge for the ten- or 12-mile float to Varney's, and you should start in the rear seat. Let your fishing partner have the better bow spot; he'll feel guilty about being in the sweet seat at the outset and will switch as soon as possible. At the end of the day you'll have had way more time up there than he will have. Fly fishing is all about prior planning and presentation, so you may as well develop the skills across the board.

One of the first tackle decisions you'll have to make is whether or not to use a dropper fly. The choice has nothing to do with sporting ethics: the Brits have condoned, even demanded, their use for centuries in revered trout lakes where each individual drift path has a formal name and an annual reservation list. Here on the Madison, the mid-stream rock you'll try to hit with a cast from the rear seat may not have as formal a name, but your guide will probably come up with one if he whacks into it with his boat. That's one reason you went with the bronc-rider: after he spits, the name he'll have for it will be *real* informal.

For starters, go with the dropper and make it a nymph that's likely to be rising today. Then tie on something bushy, high-riding and visible at the end

THE FLYCASTER

FISHING IN THE SAWTOOTH MOUNTAINS

of your leader. A Royal Trude, say, and dress it to ride like a cork. Indicator nymphing rewards focused attention, and it's even more riveting if the indicator itself sometimes draws a strike. The doubled possibilities may make the day a bit jumpy, but you've got nothing better to do, right?

Bets are off, of course, if you do catch the salmon fly hatch. Then you'll have to stout up your leader and tie on a big Number 6 dry. There are accurate new patterns for this huge stonefly, from bullet-heads to "improved," but you really ought to stick with something more classic for this greatest of Western river hatches. We're not as mired in it as the Brits, but tradition sticks to fly rods like kudzu on an Alabama billboard. There's no escaping it, even out here where the average fly fisherman learned to cast by watching a videotape and hasn't yet darkened the corks of his first fly rod. It goes back farther than that and you need to do your part. Just tie on a good old Sofa Pillow and whisper "Dan Bailey" when you cast it.

Whether you hear it or not, the river will answer.

• • •

At some point in the summer, however, each of us will have to bite the entomological bullet and do some genuine hatch-matching. There is simply no real avoiding it if we want to draw strikes from trout which are genetically predisposed and naturally selected toward eating a very specific stage of a particular insect at a given time in a certain riffle of this one river. There is no denying that if we solve the puzzle perfectly we will catch the fish.

Conventional wisdom and common sense tell us to sit down and observe the stream before tying something on and flailing away, but I've almost never been able to do this. If a Light Cahill or Adams that's about the size of the mayflies I see buzzing in the air doesn't do the job for me — or an

THE GUIDE

elk hair tie if caddis are flying — then I'm likely to call it a tough fishing day and head home, or to another piece of water. On the days that I do decide to bear down and get after them, I'll dead-drift a nymph or two, a kind of fishing that I do like even though my knowledge of which one to tie on doesn't go much past a Gold Ribbed Hare's Ear or Pheasant Tail. This year I am going to try some bead-heads.

Years ago, when I first started fly fishing, an acquaintance gave me a plastic box of flies that he had found in the attic of a dead uncle. No one in his family was a trout fisherman, said my friend, and he thought maybe I could use them.

The modern box they came in was misleading, as even in my then-novice stage I could see that these were old ties. All dry flies, none bigger than Size 12 and some down to maybe 18 or 20. I didn't know them at the time, but I now recognize that there were Cahills and Adamses, Blue Winged Olives and Hendricksons, Mosquitos, Pale Evening

Duns and a few Blue Quills. I was instantly in business, a beginner with a treasure box of beauti-fully-tied flies, and although they should have been shadow-boxed and framed, I innocently carted them instead toward trout water.

There on the stream, because I had such a broad selection to choose from without having had to think about what constituted the mix, I would take a look at what seemed to be hatching, reach into my friend's uncle's box and tie something on that roughly matched in size and color. This was purely intuitive fishing; I couldn't have told you the fly's name and it didn't matter at all to me that I couldn't. In fact, I still fish that way, still buy flies that way. Like the hunt-and-peck typing that I do every day, I've gotten pretty good at knowing which one to use and in what sequence to call for it, but I can't call the thing up by name alone. I need to see it as I use it.

Starting out the way that I did, by fumbling through my box of nameless flies and learning which ones worked only by the most rudimentary trial and error, certainly slowed my progress toward becoming a skilled hatch matcher. Stunted it, actually. It was years before I began to appreciate that knowing the difference between a caddis and a mayfly was a valuable weapon in skunk avoidance, or that smaller, darker flies weren't just a last resort after you went through all the easy-to-see lighter ones in the box. But the way that I came to learn those lessons was by learning them, not by being taught them. Like an old grouse dog who finally begins slowing to a creep at the first whiff of bird scent instead of charging headlong toward it in full lather, spooking the quarry, I've started approaching trout water with the gradually acquired knowledge that my first cast really is going to be my best chance and the correct fly is, well, the correct fly.

These lessons have come slowly not because I didn't know where to go to gather the information sooner. Quite the opposite. Since they began producing them, instructional video makers have sent me their tapes; I know how effective a teaching aid they are even though I've mostly fast-forwarded through them. I first subscribed to *Fly Fisherman* in, I think, 1972 and Art Flick and Ernie Schwiebert have been on my bookshelf for a quarter century. I have longtime friends with enough experience to write very good how-to fly fishing books; in fact, some of them have. I just haven't read them.

For a long time I wondered what sort of inertia it was that prevented me from buckling down with these learning tools and accelerating my way toward hatch matching efficiency. People I knew who had taken up fly fishing well after I did soon possessed a body of technical knowledge about the sport that was beyond mine on every level. Catalogs and fly shops sold whole books devoted to subsets of fish and insect behavior that were layers deeper than anything I could call upon in a trout stream, and expert reviewers were labeling these new volumes "indispensable," "definitive," "important" and "required reading."

A QUIET PLACE

Still, I fished without them. Year after year I kept winging it, tying on flies that seemed about right, throwing them to parts of the river that looked good to me, hoping for the best and happy with my good fortune when the trout struck. More often than not, I was surprised when they did. My expert friends, of course, were surprised when they didn't; puzzled by any uncharacteristic trout behavior, they would turn to even newer books, searching for better paradigms. It's all a science, they would say, and it can be learned. Off they would go, trending toward mastery, and leaving me even further behind.

A couple of years ago a local friend named Oliver went to New Zealand. Ollie's a dedicated outdoorsman who runs a string of Brittanies in the fall, travels routinely out of state for whitetails and is good with a fly rod. What he wanted in New Zealand was one of those torpedo-sized rainbows, and he wanted to take it from small water with a light rod. Ollie planned on being in the country for a month, and he took his buddy Stan with him. He also took a video camera.

When they got back, we all gathered at Ollie's house for a showing of the tape he and Stan made of each other. Amateur video footage of people fishing is marginal stuff no matter where it was shot, but this effort wasn't too bad, especially the bungee jump they did between rivers. Apparently it's free if you do it naked. And since I haven't been to New Zealand, I was interested in seeing the places they fished.

Their best fishing was in a river that required either a three-day hike or a helicopter ride to get to. The guide wouldn't tell them the name of the river, but promised extraordinary sight fishing for trout in excess of seven pounds. Flush with the cash they had saved on the bungee jump, Stan and Ollie opted for the helicopter and, with camera rolling, took us along for the ride.

The nameless river was more accurately labeled a stream, maybe ten yards across in its wide riffles and considerably narrower where it dropped through ancient, automobile-sized boulders in a series of short falls and deep pools where the big trout were holed up. Stan and Ollie took turns following the fully-camouflaged guide as he crept up to each holding lie and carefully scouted it for a fish. The guy who wasn't fishing ran the camcorder and whispered commentary as the other two skulked into position for a cast.

Several times during the show, Ollie would freeze-frame his VCR and point to the screen. "That's a thirty inch rainbow there. See it?" he'd say. Of course none of us could.

"That's okay," Stan would say. "We usually couldn't either. We just cast where the guide said to."

"And it wasn't easy," added Ollie. "We were using fifteen foot leaders and size twenty flies. Very technical in that clear water."

In truth it was. During an hour of video, we watched Stan and Ollie spook far more fish than they induced to rise. The fish they did hook were

all on nymphs, and they got takes only when their drifts were perfect. Rarely did they get more than two or three tries on a given fish before some infinitesimal drag would send a five pound rainbow back under its rock, an event not visible either to us in Ollie's living room or, for that matter, to whichever one of them was casting at the time. "Oops," the guide would say, "that one put him down." And off they would move to the next spot, a bit wiser and ready to try again. It wouldn't be long before the next lesson; the river seemed as full of fish as a feeder stream in a smelt run.

Ollie's best fish was a seven-pounder, a beautifully-silvered rainbow shockingly too big for the tiny pool it came out of. A fish absolutely worth traveling thousands of miles for and one that Ollie fought cautiously and well once he had hooked it on a carefully drifted Size 18 nymph directed to a deep holding lie that the guide could see from his lookout on a cross-stream boulder. The pattern was a local tie and was the only one that worked that day. A bit later in the afternoon, Stan caught one that was, if anything, bigger.

Stan and Ollie's was, in every respect, a world-class fishing trip and they came back better anglers by several orders of magnitude, armed with delicate and deadly nymphing skills too effective, almost, to use on any of the innocent little brook trout waters that flow here at home. In fact, I don't think that either of them fishes locally any more. Grant Brook was now down on the farm and they had indeed seen Par-ee.

I realized, as Becky and I drove home after the show, that I really wasn't ready to go to New Zealand, literally or figuratively. I never have wanted the expediency of having a guide show me how and when to do it, step by step right there at streamside, and my present skills certainly aren't those required to present miniature flies to educated fish in invisible water with any probability of success. This, I know, won't change very soon.

What I have always wanted from my fishing is

MORNING ON THE LAKE

FISHING THE INLET

to grow slowly with it, learning from each of the surprises that it hands individually to me. The only difference between sport fishing and commercial catching is self-induced restraint on the part of the angler, and it has always seemed to me that the more you hold back, the longer lasting your pleasure. Staying hungry is critical to longevity in any pursuit, and success assuages the appetite. Fly fishing is a lifetime's feast and I don't want to wolf my way to an overstuffed dessert while the subtle mysteries of the main course are just wafting from the kitchen.

· · ·

If you go far enough up toward Grant Brook's beginnings, up past the Skiway turnoff and out along the dirt road that skirts the last bit of pastureland before it all goes deep in timber, you can find, even on an August afternoon, enough shaded water to cast a fly to.

Dawn is the best time, of course, here in the heat of summer, but unless you're sneaking in some quality time before punching a time clock, you'll probably end up, like me, drifting out sometime after lunch with an unformulated fishing plan that calls for a quitting time around dusk. I like my fishing to start slow and get better, as it does toward dark this time of year.

The timber parcels around Grant's headwaters haven't been logged in six or eight years now, which leaves a decade or more before the old road along and occasionally across the stream will get the attention of the paper company road repair crews. The local beaver population has wised up to this inattention with a flurry of recent dam-building projects, some of them deep in the woods. The result is a series of beaver ponds that don't get sun-struck for more than an hour each day; cool, deep water brook trout havens now exist for several miles of river, all in places where just a few years ago the river ran low, slow and unobstructed all summer long. Not many of the local TU members have been up there to note the new setup, so you can pretty much have the stretch to yourself any time you want.

What you'll want, if you do arrive in the early afternoon, is some sort of ant or beetle imitation, or maybe an Ed Schenk cricket, and it'll be best fished on a nine-foot leader. Maybe you're good enough to handle something longer, but up here where the average cast is 30 feet or less, I have trouble turning a 12-footer all the way over without slapping down fly line half the time. In little streams, generating line speed is like wearing roller blades in an antique store. Go for it if you want, but be ready to pay up.

A good place to start is at the beaver dams near where Cut Brook comes in. Before the dams, maybe three years ago, this was as far upstream as you'd want to go. Above Cut Brook, Grant's isn't really trout water, but the increased flow from this point downstream is all it ever needed to hold fish all summer, and now, with the dams holding most of the

flow back, it's pretty good. Very good, actually, but we don't want this to get out. Just mumble something about slow fishing when you get back to town.

I like to fish the lowest beaver pond first. You sneak up and kneel right in the stream itself, just below the two- or three-foot-high dam. Hold back before you cast and get down as low as you can, to where you are just able to see over the dam. With your point of view right at surface level, a trout rise in that smooth water is a very cool thing to see. If the fish does it close enough, you can see the fly on the water just before it gets taken.

A very, very cool thing to see.

Okay. Now make a cast, a nice short one to this end of the pond. Easy does it. Easy... Okay. Try another, a little farther.

Nice one. Let it come back. Be ready. Be ready...

Nothing? Yeah, well, it's August. Do it again, up against the bank a bit farther out. Maybe an extra false cast—

Tree branch behind you. To be expected, really. It's the shade up here that keeps the fishing alive this time of year; we'll be dodging limbs all day. I hope you can roll cast that long leader you tied on. I usually end up with spaghetti.

After an hour or so, we won't have a fish. It's still early and hot, so I'll put on something smaller. Last year in Michigan, Becky and I stopped by a fly shop in Traverse City and I almost bought a pair of fishing glasses that had the little bifocal magnifying inserts in them. Becky vetoed the acquisition, saying they were "geeky." I asked her how she thought any of us looked in baggy rubber pants and headnets with little metal and plastic gizmos pinned to our pockets.

In any case the answer really is to downsize, and it can become genuinely annoying. The tiny flies are hard to deal with, difficult to see on the water, and the ultra-skinny tippets don't hold up at all well to errant passages through alder thickets and pine boughs. In an August afternoon's fishing

STRIPER COUNTRY

I'll spend fully half my time rerigging something: a fly that doesn't draw any response; a tippet that thought it was a bull whip; wind knots; fly floatant that I accidentally put on a nymph; a Size 24 hook that broke when I tried to pinch down the barb. The sun will have been hot on my neck at times and in my eyes at others. Tiny half-finished clinch knots will turn into microscopic Gordians. Or frictionless grannies that slip off hook eyes time after time as I test them. Trying to pick a new Size 20 from my fly box, I'll have three others stick to my sweaty fingers and then drop, instantly invisible, into the flowing water at my feet.

That's about the point when I'd happily chuck it all for an instant transport to a Nantucket beach in the high surf, with a 12-foot spinning rod and a half-pound lure sprouting treble hooks that I could heave with everything I've got straight into a gale toward an oceanful of slashing, slamming bluefish and striped bass duking each other out in a muscular, predatory frenzy, trying desperately to chomp

the hook so I can lean hard against the hammering fight and drag a ten-pounder thrashing and tooth-snapping up onto the hissing, foaming beach . . .

Whoa. Easy, guy. Take a seat there and listen to the forest birds. Close your eyes and let the sweet gurgle of the brook wash all that nasty stuff away. So what if you haven't caught one yet? Where would you rather be, at work?

The restorative powers of a few carefully drawn breaths on the edge of a trout stream with the rest of the day ahead of you can be miraculous, don't you think?

Well, hey. The sun's dipping now. There'll be some sort of hatch any time now. What do you say we sit here and wait for it? It's sure to be a small caddis and the brookies will start to rise right over there in that slickwater run past the overhanging spruce tree. We can wait right here.

What's the hurry?

• • •

STREAM THROUGH THE FARMLAND

*L*ately I've been thinking about the Madison River. You know what it's like; maybe you've been on it. Rich water, big country: the definition of Paradise for some of the more serious fishermen I know.

It's a river of attributes, and high on that list is the fact that you know what it is. Where it is. What swims in it. And, if you read a bit, who fishes it when, and with what success. You know these things, or most of them, because the Madison is...

Here's where I've been getting bogged down a bit.

I know that you can go there, and that you can fish in the beauty of Yellowstone, or further downstream in the big water of the west side. You can cast dry flies in long glides or toss muddlers on stiff leaders to wild spawning brown trout in the fall. In the spring there will be broods of Canada geese and the singing of thrush in the aspens, and as the season passes, you will share the beaver meadows with elk and moose and river otters, and

you will stand thigh deep in the moving heart of preserved wild fishing in America.

But I also know this: It's a place without secrets.

Go to a Trout Unlimited or Theodore Gordon meeting and someone will say, drink in his hand, after his introduction by your friend Walt, "When were you last on the Madison?"

If you shrug and let out that it's been five or ten years or, possibly, that you've never fished it, you'll get a blank look. "Really?" he'll say. "Well you get yourself to West Yellowstone and tell them I sent you. Ask for..."

Or, easier yet, go to the books and magazines and look for it. It will be there, flowing smooth blue out of the Firehole and across the pages. There will be fly casters there and they will be happy to tell you when to fish, and how. And why. And... and they will be right. They'll even be right about the "why." For the river is for real; just look at it.

As the man said: it just doesn't get any better

than this. And it's there for all and each of us, whenever we want it. If you haven't, you ought to do it. I ought to to do it again, and I will.

In fact the only reason that I haven't been back sooner is that these other little places keep getting in the way. Places that you don't know much about.

One of them is a small rock. Worn granite, I think. Up north. You can sit on it with your wader feet in the current and around behind you from the left comes a feeder brook.

If you sit there, the first you'll notice is the water sound — trill, trill, trill-a and the occasional gurgle — and a bit later you'd realize that there is a wind rustle in the maples and chickadees in the alders. Nothing new there; I'm sure you'd notice it right away, picking it all out from experience and times alone in other places.

But if you were, for a minute, me, there would be something else. A part of you would be slipping upstream in the feeder, past the first rundown beaver dams and around the spruce hillocks to the open hardwoods where the stream runs roundabout for two miles and then ends — starts, really — in the seepage emanating from the slip-slide jumble of the rock wall that marks the true beginning of Number Three Mountain.

The true beginning of Number Three Mountain. And the beginning of other things, too, not so easily marked. Just over to the east (hard to measure distance here in the deep woods, in the leaf-cover of fishing time) is where the moose bed down in November, uphill from where you saw the bear track last year, and a good distance to the west of where you had been three years before when you thought that the road should have been near but it wasn't and you kept moving on a compass line, very much in doubt for the last twenty minutes, and moving, moving south until there it was and then you could actually feel the woods rotating around you as your mind reset itself to the very plain reality of a road running exactly 90 degrees different than you had thought it would be just the minute before.

The little brook that now cools your feet could take you there quickly, and you know it now as you sit. And you know other things — that the brook flows down to camp, to a tent sitting on the bared spot where it has come and gone six seasons now. There are markers there. Oaken tent pegs broken off deep in the dirt in cold seasons, and rock-dams in the spring flowage where beer cooled in other Junes, other Septembers. And voices, loud with today and fading muted from before. Sitting here now, on the rock — it is granite, it's so quiet — you can strain to reach forward for the voices to come. Hear them? Hear them? No . . . ?

No, I can't hear them, either. Not now. That will come when they come. For now, I'll stay here, in this brook, downstream from what went before, upcurrent from what's coming next. I'm going to tie on a dry fly, and I'm going to cast it up to before and watch it drift to the future. Maybe a tiny

brook trout will dismantle this little piece of time in its passage.

And all the while, and later at night in the tent, white pine whisper overhead, I'll wonder: Can you have this on the Madison River? Does it work there so neatly as it does in the unknown places, or does your Number Six Goofus Bug time machine collide with the bumpy passage of other memories and plans, other's memories. And plans.

I don't know.

. . .

That trout can remain hidden in the deeper and wider courses of a full-sized river seems as natural to the observer as blue sky and green water, but the complete invisibility of those same fish in an ankle-deep rivulet where individual stones stand out clearly on the bottom is something almost mystical. All of the life on this planet has come from

THE EDGE OF THE RIVER

the water, and on a small brook at the right moment, when a four-inch brook trout suddenly moves from its holding station, it can seem to happen as you watch.

Hey, Fred. Come over here. There are fish *in this thing.*

Standing beside a long, smooth stretch of the Madison or the Umpqua, or even near the more intimate runs of something like the Au Sable in Michigan, you expect to see trout rising, and if you are actually fishing, then it's a genuine disappointment each time a clean float turns to downstream drag without some sort of strike. You know the fish are there, down in the depths where you can't see them. But in a tiny stream, a seasonal feeder or one of those little Appalachian freestones that hikers can easily get across with dry feet, the snap of a feeding trout on your just-presented fly can be as shocking as the outcome of that back-of-the-boat chumming scene in *Jaws*. If the Yellowstone had proportionately sized trout to those in a mountain brook, you'd be using marlin tackle to land them. From the shore, where you'd be safe.

Fishing alone on a small stream forces you to shrink yourself, literally and figuratively. Most of the ones I've fished are tightly overhung with trees, alders and other impedimenta that require a short line and cautious back cast to avoid hangups, and the riffles and pools themselves are small enough that if you ever did throw a 60-foot cast most of your fly line would fall on top of the two or three good spots between you and your leader that you should be targeting instead. And it's hard to carry much personal grandiosity when you're hunkered on your knees in running water, trying to dap an ant-sized lure just over a rock ten feet away in the hopes of tricking a five-inch trout.

On the other hand, maybe it's hard not to. After all, there aren't many of us who really want this kind of angling. Or who understand why it's so satisfying.

For two years in a row Becky and I took our children to Ennis, Montana over the Fourth of July.

We stayed with Pete and Ginny Combs at their beautiful Diamond J dude ranch just outside of town, up toward the Spanish Peaks and nestled along Jack Creek. During our week there, we'd ride up into the mountains after cutthroats one day, drive down to the Madison for a float on the next, and go to town for the rodeo and parade on the Fourth itself.

One day, on our second trip, my bad knee had swelled up from the previous day's long ride, and I stayed at the ranch while everyone else either went back up into the mountains or down to the big river. I sat on the porch of our cabin drinking coffee, reading a yellow-edged Mickey Spillane from the bookshelf and glassing a small band of mountain goats on the rocky peaks south of the ranch. By early afternoon I'd had enough black coffee and purple prose ("...I pulled the trigger and his hands disappeared in a nightmare of blue holes..."). My knee was feeling better, so I strung my five-weight and wandered down to Jack Creek.

The sun was high and the sky clear, but there was enough shade from streambank trees to keep the water cool, especially at this elevation. The only bugs coming off were a few desultory caddis and the occasional midge that meant nothing to me. I tied on a Royal Trude, maybe a size 14, and flipped a little roll cast up the bank. Nothing. I tried it again. Nope.

Splip! There was a splashy little rise right where the fly had been. I switched to a smaller elk hair caddis, about size 18, and made another cast. I mended slightly as the fly came back at me, past the spot and *Splip!* Strike. Hooked. A fat little rainbow, maybe nine inches. Cool, I thought. This will do just fine.

For the next hour and a half I worked slowly up the stream, past the ranch buildings and into a narrower, more densely wooded stretch of the valley. In the shaded pools there weren't very many takers, but when I came back out into an alpine meadow I could see mayflies backlit by the afternoon sun where the stream wound slowly through

THROUGH THE WHITEWATER

the open, waist-high grasses. It was maybe three o'clock. I had hours to spend right here on this pristine little stream, and I wondered if I might find a cutthroat this far down out of the mountains themselves and just a short walk from the road.

Here in the meadow, the creek wound through a series of tight S-turns and it was hard to find a place to make a long enough cast to get any sort of drift. Instead I had to roll cast and dap, even out here in the treeless open, but the fish were there and they were feeding. Almost all rainbows and the occasional hybrid showing a faint red slash under its mouth, none anywhere near 12 inches.

At the head of the meadow, the creek came out of a tight little canyon in a series of low falls marked by rocky steps and ancient, almost petrified trees that had come down in spring runoffs to wedge into corners and form dams that redirected the flow through deep troughs and narrow fastwater runs. Almost perfect trout water.

I started at the bottom and soon found what is still my all-time favorite trout fishing situation. In a half-circle of granite steps and tree-dams, the creek wound down and around me in three cascading pools, each within perfect casting range. The topmost one was almost at eye level, smooth as glass and 20 feet across with at least six fish regularly rising in it. If you can imagine your best little dry fly run with a shoulder-deep pit dug for you so that you could walk right up to it and cast standing up to fish rising at eye level 30 feet away and completely unaware of your presence, then you've got what I found on Jack Creek that afternoon.

I spent an hour there, maybe more. After I caught the first one, a seven-inch rainbow, the top pool went dead for a while. So I cast to the lower pool until one of those fish hit. Then down to the lowest. By the time I had one from there, the top pool was back in action. I didn't even have to move my feet, except to step carefully over and release one of the little trout. It was a magic show.

And then it ended, almost instantly when the

sun tipped behind a peak and dropped a cold shadow on the water. I tried different patterns for a while, but it was over. I didn't mind. I reeled in, clipped off and unstrung.

On my way back through the meadow, heading down toward the ranch and wondering whether or not Spillane knew that a Mickey Finn was a streamer, I almost stepped on a mule deer fawn. It's the only time I've ever seen one like that, all curled up in the grass with its white-spotted coat and ears laid back, not looking at me and absolutely without motion. I looked around for the doe, but she was not to be seen. I don't think the little deer was a couple of days old.

Down in the main lodge, people had started to gather for drinks and dinner, their talk full of high horse trails and hitting the pocket water from drift boats down on the Madison.

"You missed a great ride today," someone said.

"I'll bet," I answered. "Must have been able to see forever from up there today."

"How's the old knee?" someone else asked. "Going to able to get out tomorrow, or you stuck with the Jack Creek minnows again?"

My knee felt great. I hadn't thought about it all day.

"I'm not sure," I said. "I think it still hurts."

• • •

SALMON FISHERMEN

ATLANTIC SALMON

Casting a fly to an Atlantic salmon in fresh water is like extending your hand to the Princess of Monaco at a formal charity ball. Your invitation to dance may reflect a set of intentions ranging from timidly social to amorously hopeful, but in the very unlikely event that she does decide to waltz with you, her bored acceptance will spring without thought from years of prior training and not in the least because she actually thinks that your proffered arm is something she wants to take.

The dedicated Atlantic salmon fishermen I know are not at all put off by this reticence. It is, in fact, a major part of the attraction. For most of them the point is to be in the ballroom in the first place, either because they are very good dancers who have worked hard to get here, or because they just love the ceremony and tradition of it all even if they don't know whether the current music calls for a minuet or a tango. And by God have you ever seen anything as beautiful as the princess herself?

HOLDING AT THE POOL

The last couple of summers in the Maritime Provinces of Canada have had long periods of drought followed by spates of rain. As a result, picking a week to go salmon fishing has been a true lottery, and Becky and I came up dry two years in a row on our regular visit with Charles and Patricia Gaines in Nova Scotia. We dealt with the low-water problem by heading inland and fishing for smallmouth bass in lakes, and by driving down to the coast and casting to salmon in the estuaries where they held, waiting for the next cold flush of fresh, rain-produced water to draw them upstream to spawn.

At the mouth of the Salmon River there is a fairly permanent gravel bar onto which you can drive at any tide and join the other salmon fishermen trying for the hundreds of fresh fish gathered there. In droughts like the one Becky and I found ourselves in, when there are no fish at all in the upper reaches of the local rivers, there will be a dozen or three serious Atlantic salmon fishermen on the gravel bar, politely forming a slow moving line and rhythmically covering the hundred yards or so of fishable water. On a Saturday morning in August, Charles's friend Dave Clark took us down there.

It's disconcerting to see so many fine fly casters packed closely together like that, especially when you know that each of them would rather have been completely alone and nowhere near here, where they found themselves fishing in a venue far better suited to pyramid sinkers and live bait flung with spinning gear. As we strung up our rods, Dave wandered down to talk to a friend who was already fishing.

"There was a bit of a flurry at first light, right when the tide changed," Dave reported back to us. "Nothing in the last hour or so. My friend's had a couple of looks at a dry, though."

While we watched, a bright fish did just that, rolling a flash of silver in the deep current near the man's bright green Bomber. The fisherman turned to us and shrugged; the other casters didn't miss a

MORNING ON THE MIRAMICHI

TAKING LINE

beat. Apparently salmon had been doing that all morning. No surprise, really, with them fresh from the ocean and so energy-laden.

In turn, we joined the casting queue. The drill was to wait until the angler in front of you had moved ten yards or so downstream before you took his place at the end of the line, about a hundred yards upstream from the rocky beach. The fisherman who had reached the mouth would control the rate of change by deciding when to give it up and rotate back to the end, freeing the rest of the line to move down a notch. There was an identical operation on the other side of the stream. Call it two dozen flies in the water at any given moment, each swinging across and down in front of what had to be a large number of salmon and grilse.

It was a beautiful thing to watch, especially when you were sitting it out, waiting for your turn to reenter the line. A fly line in the air over flowing water may be as elegant a visual image as the sporting life can present to an onlooker. These were high backcasts and tight loops thrown by long-experienced casters who knew that people were watching. In this company, Becky and I would have ranked at the bottom of the meet had someone been holding up score cards.

We fished for an hour or two that way, and no one even tickled one. I did the depressing arithmetic: Figure four casts per minute for each angler, two dozen people throwing a wide variety of fly patterns at great numbers of visibly active salmon. Thousands of casts by very good anglers who were paying attention. Nothing. I wondered how the odds would have changed had we been there to feed ourselves, if we'd been heaving metal instead of feathers, looking for dinner. The beach would have been littered with caught fish, I knew. It would have been too easy. But that, of course, was exactly why we were all fly fishing.

Becky finally hooked one, a nice-sized grilse that immediately went airborne, surged across the stream, jumped again and broke off. It was the only

THE GUIDE AND THE SPORT

fish hooked in the three or four hours we were there. With all those flies dead drifting and riffle-hitching past that many salmon, someone certainly had to hook up sometime and even if the fish got so quickly away, I was glad it was Becky.

But if you think it improbable that the fish ate Becky's fly and not one so stylishly delivered by one of the much better casters standing on either side of her, then you haven't spent much time on an Atlantic salmon river.

. . .

The George River drains a vast tundra-swathed wilderness in northern Quebec, flowing almost due north into Ungava Bay with a volume of undammed water that is many times greater than its hydroelec-tric-hobbled little cousins to the south. Saved so far from the engineers and concrete-pourers by the bothersome economics of having to pay for all those miles and miles of transmission line to get the juice from Eskimo caribou barrens to American home entertainment centers, the impassive and relentless George is a good salmon river in the sense that the Autobahn is a fine road. It certainly is, but you do want to be ready when you get on it.

Becky and I, along with our friend André Croteau from Montreal, floated down 100 miles of the George in an inflatable boat, camping for a week along the way and hoping to intercept the first salmon of the year as they swam toward us. We started on the first of July; the ice had been off the water for ten days.

Putting in at a wide, deep section of river called Indian House Lake, we waved goodbye to the French-speaking bush pilot who had hauled us up there from the end of the railroad line at Schefferville. He had agreed to come find us in a week, somewhere downriver. André expected that the take out spot would be at another good float-plane location called Wedge Hills; we had good maps and André had floated the river before. Off we went in glorious, sunny weather.

Within a few hours we were into fish. Lake trout and pike, and a few big brook trout. No salmon, but we hadn't expected any to have made it this far upriver yet. That night we pitched camp among caribou tracks and huge chunks of leftover winter ice that was glacial blue and scattered under the sun-shielding bluffs where a little creek had cut its way into the big river. Sometime after midnight a wolf howled and I got up to look around. Daylight had not completely surrendered up here just a few parallels beneath the true midnight sun; there was no wind and the only sound was the endless, ancient hiss of all that water before me, sliding north.

For the next four days we alternated between long, flat stretches and headlong, shrieking pitches down haystack chutes of surging rapids. At the foot of each piece of fastwater we'd beach the boat, rearrange the load, dry ourselves off and string up our rods. If the place seemed like good holding water, or if we just needed the heat, we'd build a driftwood fire. If we could in fact find wood; trees are rare and distant up there, but the receding backwaters of spring runoff leave small collections of gatherable branches.

In none of the these places did we find a fresh salmon. On the second day we did take a lethargic black salmon, maybe fifteen pounds, but we were looking for the silver and we put it back.

We got to Wedge Hills the afternoon before the plane was due, and the next morning we deflated the boat, packed all our gear and waited. Bush pilots are, well, bush pilots, and they live by the wind on various levels. We knew this, of course, so we didn't think much of it when the floatplane failed to appear that day. Tomorrow, then.

The next day, while we waited, the caribou appeared. First as distant silhouettes on the tundra hills far across the river, and then as tiny moving shapes, the individual animals coalesced into a herd as they flowed downhill and into the river itself.

Riding high in the current, they swam across as if they were walking, and they began to come ashore a half mile upstream from us. There the caribou would shake off the cold water and trot off immediately, making room on the bank for those behind them. There were thousands of them, a river of animals as indifferent to us as they were to the ground itself as they passed over it. We guessed that there were 25,000 of them, a smaller subset of the half-million that make up the largest caribou herd in North America.

As the day waned, with no floatplane appearing, we decided to fish. Unpacking our rods and walking a mile or so downriver from our gear, we cast into a marginal-looking pool and within five minutes André had a bright fish on. It leaped immediately, a 15-pound male with the kype beginning to show in its jaw. A few minutes later Becky took a hen fish, and before she could land it, I hooked another a hundred yards downstream from her.

We took a dozen fish in the two hours before the floatplane appeared, all bright fish and all within a quarter mile of where André took the first one. They had to be the lead pod of this year's salmon run, a hundred miles up from the ocean, arriving with the tilting solstice, and we had almost missed them.

But we didn't. We were there and we touched them, just barely and for an instant, a hundred miles down from where we started and only an hour or two from being lifted, up and away and over the flowing caribou, back to the courses of our regular lives.

• • •

TROLLING IN THE ADIRONDACKS

FALL

FISHING BELOW THE OLD DAM

RIVER REFLECTIONS

FALL

*Meanwhile
let us cast one shadow
in air or water.*
—Maxine Kumin

September on Grant Brook is a time to stand on the bank and just look at it. The variegated yellows and browns of the freestone streambed begin to meld visually with the turning maples, ash and beeches reflected from above onto the flowing surface, and the water itself grows daily clearer, freeing itself of sun-bred algaes and the clouded minutiae of microscopic lives that breed in the convected waters of high summer.

At this time of year, each night resets the next day's fishing. Chilling both the air and the water from their combined frenetics of the previous afternoon, a September night sky will try literally to draw the breath out of Grant Brook, pulling the stream's heated, living soul up from the earth and out toward the Milky Way in the cycle that faces us all, lifting life's durable specific and spewing it into the dissipating eternal.

Do it now, whispers Grant Brook as it grows colder. *Do it now.*

Both species of fall-spawning trout — brookies and browns — heed the call, but the brook trout don formal wear. By mid September

A SMALL STREAM

121

In the Fall

they've taken on a glorious glow, dressing them-selves in sharpened blues hued with orange and etched with the brightened ivory of their leading edges as if the flowing brook itself has become a sort of warped parade ground and you are there to review and inspect their best vestments.

But you've got to catch them first, and you can only do that if you don't waste any chances to get out on the water, especially here in New England where an errant Arctic air mass can put down the action like headlights on a midnight skinny dip.

A September day on Grant Brook doesn't have to be a dawn patrol, but on the other hand there's no reason not to be out there early. There are several miles of hiking paths and logging roads that parallel the water and if you don't mind wan-dering the back country in your felt soles, you can begin the day in the best way possible, by walking slowly into it. I like to pack a pair of flyweight hippers and light wading shoes in my old green daypack and plan on spending as much of the day in sneakers on the trail as in water itself. You might be tempted to skip the extra gear and fish the little stream by wading wet, but I'd caution you against it. Every time I've tried it I've caught myself getting out of the water to warm up when I should really be hanging in a bit longer, warm and dry in the hippers and felts. One more cast might have done it, right?

We'll park my Jeep at the first turnout. That will leave a half mile of walking before we get to the brook, but if you don't mind I'd really prefer to start that way rather than by driving right down to the water. Modern sport seems every year to lie just the other side of increasingly easy to open portals, and I don't think we've elevated the game by bring-ing it so close to the commerce of our daily lives. It's good to walk a bit between the two, better if you do it alone, and best with a quiet friend who knows the distance.

Come on. I'll show you what I mean. Maybe

we'll see a moose along the way, and if you know your warblers you'll probably get a good count. Any luck at all and we'll hear a hermit thrush, but chances of that really are better earlier in the season. The grouse out here seem to drum right up till bird season; I don't know why.

Walk slowly. We'll listen together.

Just above the beaver impoundments on Grant Brook are the stone foundations of an old mill, or some other 19th century enterprise. I don't know the history of it, but I've guessed from poking around the ruins that it was some sort of combined logging sluice and water mill. Maybe you've studied these things and can tell me about it while we fish the slow bend behind the place. It's good dry fly water, knee-deep for most of its length, but silty on the bottom near the end of the run; we'll have to take some care there if we plan on fishing down-stream afterward.

When I first discovered the stoneworks, they discomforted me. You can't really see them from the road, and I had started to cut through what I thought was a low patch of old spruces and cedars. A century or more of flooding silt and dropping needles had filled in the cellar holes and collapsed doorways, and I didn't realize what I was standing in until the rectangular forms of the place presented themselves to me in a sudden gestalt that came up from my subconscious like a dark wind on the back of my neck. I stopped, looked around, and then hurried out into the sunlight where the brook flowed past, purling softly and blue as baby's eyes.

It took me a while, standing in the bright water and casting with the sun on my back, to regain the Tom-and-Huck-playing-hooky tone that a day on Grant Brook usually carries. It felt effete and disconnected with the granite past of northern New England to be playing here in the stone remains of lost labor, standing in the water in my nylon-laminate pants, delicately waving a graphite four-weight and searching for six-inch trout through UV-protecting polaroid sunglasses. But the discomfort came

only from me, and only for a short while; the sagging stones of the old buildings carried no echoes from the old men and they said nothing themselves. They were, in fact, receding contentedly back to where they had been, bedrock for the green growth and running flood of the living things that tripped lightly over them, year to year, century to century, aeon to aeon.

I felt better then. I was right back where I was supposed to be, where I had meant to go, standing in the river and deflecting the cold, content to be flittingly alive and happy to be wanting something that I knew was there but couldn't quite see.

Today, though, we might actually see them. A brook trout's ivory-tipped fins stand out nicely against a tannic bottom, especially here in the fall when they're in spawning colors. Let's separate and fish apart for an hour or so. That way we can each concentrate — or not, for that matter — and fish just the way we want to. You probably want to set your own pace, and I know I want to regulate mine.

THE LAKE IN THE FALL

At this stage of the angling season, with so much behind and so little ahead, I really don't want to mess with anything that doesn't carry some spiritual weight. For me, fishing passed long ago from diversion to requisite and now, faced with winter's dark entropic, I want each cast genuinely to count. You accomplish that, I've finally decided, not by learning how to throw a line, but by knowing when not to. On the September trout stream, none of us is any longer just a boy, giving it all away; it's time now to select a fly, and to place it on the water only when it ought to be there.

Some of my deeply-into-it fly fishing friends have tried to explain to me how closely this latter stage of expertise can come to the state sought by a Zen archer as he meditates toward the extinction of his desires and strives to become the arrow itself, unerrant toward the cosmic bull's eye of achieved selflessness, but I haven't bought into the analogy. A refined angler doesn't deny his cravings, he focuses them. Even in his most ascetic catch-and-release postures, there is simply too much hunger in any angler's quest for a fish. Every one of us, after all, wants a tight line. The only difference is what we wish for at the end, and how we touch it when it's there.

And so, aging with the cooling waters that surround us, we each begin to channel more and more of our days into directed retrieves and away from random casts. Taking increasing measures of joy from the elusive process and less from the wriggling result, we find ourselves fishing as much in our minds as in the actual waters at our feet. There, in the clarified light of autumn, as the angled brightness of the sun shines unshadowed by the fallen leaves of summer into the almost invisible river that calls us,

that draws us,

that pulls us,

we want, at last, simply to be there.

• • •

WINTER ON THE STREAM